HARVARD LECTURES ON
THE VERGILIAN AGE

LONDON : HUMPHREY MILFORD

OXFORD UNIVERSITY PRESS

HARVARD LECTURES ON
THE VERGILIAN AGE

BY

ROBERT SEYMOUR CONWAY

Litt.D. (Cantab.), Hon.D.Litt. (Oxon.), Hon.Litt.D. (Dub.), Hon.Dott.Univ. (Padua)
Fellow of the British Academy
Hulme Professor of Latin in the University of Manchester
Hon. Fellow of Gonville and Caius College, Cambridge
Recently Visiting Lecturer in Harvard University

CAMBRIDGE

HARVARD UNIVERSITY PRESS

1928

PRINTED AT THE HARVARD UNIVERSITY PRESS

CAMBRIDGE, MASS., U. S. A.

TO

CLIFFORD HERSCHEL MOORE, Ph.D., Litt.D.

My dear Clifford Moore,
While I was the guest of Harvard, I was greeted every
day at the gate by two lines of Horace:

Felices ter et amplius,
Quos inrupta tenet copula,

a benediction which I took as an omen of our own friendship.
And since it was through your generous encouragement that
these lectures were delivered and are published in Harvard,
I claim for them now, so long as they may last, the honour
of being linked with your name.

In grateful regard yours,

R. S. CONWAY

Manchester, England
March, 1928

PREFACE

THE nine lectures in this volume may be regarded as a continuation of my *New Studies of a Great Inheritance*, published in 1921. They are concerned with the life of about forty years (55–17 B.C.), a period which, in spite of political vicissitudes, has a unity of its own, the true golden age of Roman literature; and they will, I hope, serve to show that its governing conceptions are represented most clearly by Vergil, so that it may be naturally called the Vergilian Age.

The purpose of this volume differs somewhat from that of the *Great Inheritance*. What I have here tried to do is to identify the elements in the feeling of the time which shaped, or coloured, the thought of its great writers. This involved some new study of its historical conditions, but my object was not to describe those conditions, which are, for the most part, well known, — if one can use the phrase of anything in ancient history, — but rather to discover what the poets and historians really felt about them. Thus the second lecture, though it is an essay in topographic research, suggests questions of another kind: What did Vergil feel about his first home? And how did he judge the events by which he lost it? It is the atmosphere round the authors which we ought to breathe again if we are to understand their work; and this may be often felt less clearly in what they wrote explicitly about the incidents of that day than in their reflections on other events, some of them remote in time, or even wholly imaginary. For example, the Hannibalic War, though it ended a century and a half before Vergil's generation, nevertheless was clearly present to it as a sombre historical picture. And what Vergil's contemporaries felt about the different aspects of that war was closely linked with their own experience. If this was so, we shall not fully understand what they wrote unless we have realised this connexion.

From this point of view the different chapters contribute to a single purpose; nevertheless they may be found useful, one by one, as in fact they were written. They are arranged in what I believe to be the chronological order in which the parts of Roman literature with which they are chiefly concerned were first written. Thus, for example, the third lecture, though its topic is taken from Book VI of the *Aeneid*, is intended chiefly to make clear the new light which flashed out upon the world of 40 B.C. in Vergil's Fourth Eclogue. The next lecture is concerned with a prosaic but still significant incident of 36 B.C. One accidental, but perhaps not inconvenient, result of this arrangement is that the lectures on parts of Livy's work and other documents in prose alternate with those devoted to Vergil, save that the second combines both kinds of evidence.

Five of the lectures were delivered as part of a public course on Vergil in Harvard University last spring; among them is the seventh, which contains the fullest statement of the views for which I am most concerned to plead. All the other lectures were implied and some were actually given, though in a less formal shape, as part of the Graduate and other Courses for which I was responsible in that half-year. But it is hardly necessary to add that the work on which they were based was begun long before 1927. Most of the lectures had taken shape, in one form or another, as part of my work at Manchester since 1920; and I am indebted to the kindness of the editors of the *John Rylands Library Bulletin* and of *Discovery*, who have allowed me to use freely a good deal of matter which has appeared from time to time in those periodicals. My best thanks are also due to the Harvard University Press for its kind offer to publish the volume; and to their senior press-reader, whose thoughtful criticism has removed not a few obscurities. I have further to express my gratitude to my distinguished friend and former pupil, Professor J. Whatmough, Fellow of the American Academy, for his great kindness in seeing the prefatory and index matter through the press, during my absence on a visit to the Universities of Australia and New Zealand, for which I am now embarked.

R. S. C.

S. S. Remeura, Panama Canal, *July, 1928*

CONTENTS

   I. The Proscription of 43 b.c. 3

  II. Where was Vergil's Farm? . ✓ 14

 III. The Golden Bough ⚵ 41

 IV. The House of the High Priest 54

  V. An Unnoticed Aspect of Vergil's Personality . 63

 VI. Under Hannibal's Shadow 73

 VII. The Philosophy of Vergil ✓ 94

VIII. The Portrait of a Roman Noble 113

 IX. The Architecture of the Epic 129

Index of Proper Names 153

Index of Topics discussed 158

List of Passages cited from Vergil 161

ILLUSTRATIONS

1. THE MANTUAN DISTRICT 14

2. MANTUA AS IT IS 16

3. OROGRAPHIC PLAN OF THE MANTUAN DISTRICT . . . 28

4. PIETOLE 28

5. WAYSIDE STREAM NEAR CARPENEDOLO 30

6. WAYSIDE STREAM, WITH A SMALL SLUICE, NEAR CAR-
   PENEDOLO 30

7. THE RIDGE OF CARPENEDOLO. 32

8. THE BELL-TOWER OF CALVISANO 34

9. THE BELL-TOWER OF S. ANDREA, MANTUA 34

10. THE RIVER MELLA 36

11. THE RIVER CHIESE (CLESIS), BETWEEN CARPENEDOLO
    AND CALVISANO 36

12. THE BRESCIAN ALPS SEEN FROM CALVISANO . . . 38

13, 14. NEW FRAGMENTS OF FASTI 54

15. THE REGIA RESTORED 56

16. THE POSITION OF THE FRAGMENTS 58

THE VERGILIAN AGE

I

THE PROSCRIPTION OF 43 B.C.

MOST people at some time or other have read Shakespeare's *Julius Caesar*. But one scene in it, which is grim enough when its meaning comes home to us, is apt to pass away quickly from the memory, because it is rather isolated where it stands in the play. I mean the few lines in Act IV in which Antony, Octavius, and Lepidus confer about the Proscription.

Ant. These many, then, shall die; their names are pricked.
Oct. Your brother too must die; consent you, Lepidus?
Lep. I do consent —
Oct. Prick him down, Antony.
Lep. Upon condition Publius shall not live,
    Who is your sister's son, Mark Antony.
Ant. He shall not live; look, with a spot I damn him.

The object of this lecture is to sketch some aspects of life in Italy during that reign of terror, partly by the help of an inscription which was anciently engraved on marble at Rome, and of which a not unimportant part has been recently discovered.

Several large fragments of marble containing what appears to be the eulogy of a husband upon his wife had long been known [1] in Rome, although unluckily only two of the fragments themselves are preserved, the rest being known to us from copies made after the first discovery. But in 1898 another fragment was found, the contents of which clearly showed that they belonged to the same monument. The inscription is an authentic piece of Roman literature, unique in its kind. The style of the writing and the contents alike make it certain that it was set up in the time of Augustus; but the whole offered a kind of missing-word puzzle, because the first few lines, which no doubt contained the names of the people

---

[1] *Corpus Inscriptionum Latinarum*, VI, 1527 and 31670.

whom it concerned, were broken away and lost, so that the inscription was (and is) like a dog that has eaten his label; we could not tell to whom it was to be ascribed. No part of the surviving fragments gives us either the name of the husband or the name of the wife he mourns, though they tell us a great deal else about them. But the historian Appian, who wrote in Greek in the second century A.D., included in Book IV of his *History of the Civil Wars* some details of the Proscription of 43 B.C., and scholars have been able to pick out from these a particular Roman noble called Quintus Lucretius Vispullo, whose story tallies with that of the monument. The same story is recorded more briefly by Valerius Maximus,[1] who gives the wife's name as Turia.

Vispullo, then, it was who engraved on marble, at what must have been great cost, a biography of the wife with whom he had lived, as he tells us, for forty-one years, and thanks to whom he had escaped the deadly peril of having been put upon the list of the proscribed. But before we turn to Turia herself, we must try to form some conception of what that proscription was.

After the murder of Julius Caesar on the Ides of March, 44 B.C., Mark Antony seized on all his papers and property; and by his eloquent speech to the people drove Brutus and Cassius and the other conspirators into what was almost exile in Asia Minor, while he departed to govern (and tax) the provinces of Gaul. The Senate hesitated, but at length, roused by Cicero and supported by Octavian, Caesar's heir, a youth of nineteen who as yet held no political office, decided that Antony's pretensions must be resisted. Accordingly the two consuls, Hirtius and Pansa, with Octavian, raised an army and defeated Antony at Mutina (the modern Modena) in North Italy in April, 43 B.C.; but Hirtius and Pansa fell in the battle, and Antony and Octavian at once made terms with one another and with Lepidus, another general who was in command of an army in the north. One of the conditions on which their compact was formed, a compact generally known as the Second

---

[1] In Book VI, 72, of his collection of 'Memorable Deeds and Words,' dedicated to the Emperor Tiberius (A.D. 14–37).

Triumvirate, was the Proscription, by which each secured the death, and the confiscation of all the property, of his particular enemies. This list was agreed upon by Antony, Lepidus, and Octavian, at two long sittings, Octavian having at first resisted Antony's demand for the death of Cicero, with whom he, Octavian, had been in most friendly relations since his return to Rome after Caesar's death. However, Octavian gave way, and the Triumvirs marched to Rome at the head of their armies and proclaimed peace; but the first act of the peace was to set up a list of persons — very few of whom had taken part in the Civil Wars or in politics, but all of whom were wealthy — who were to be hunted to death like beasts.

The actual words of the proclamation have been preserved by Appian. Nothing could give a clearer picture of what the Roman world must have looked like when Vergil was twenty-seven years old than this strange document, which marks the end of the first scene of Octavian's public career.

We, Marcus Lepidus, Marcus Antonius, and Octavius Caesar, having been elected to bring into harmony and order the affairs of the Republic, make the following proclamation. But for the treachery with which disloyal citizens, who had obtained mercy when they prayed for it, nevertheless became enemies of him who had shown them kindness and conspired against his life, Gaius Julius Caesar would never have been slain by those whom he took prisoners in war and mercifully spared and whom, one and all, he had treated as friends and promoted to honours; nor should we now be compelled to take these measures against all those who have insulted us and proclaimed us public enemies. But as things are, seeing that the wickedness of those who have plotted to destroy us, and by whom Caesar was slain, cannot be overcome by any kindness, we choose to anticipate our enemies rather than to suffer ourselves. Therefore let no man think us guilty of unjust or cruel excesses, when he remembers the fate of Caesar and the wrongs[1] that have been done to us. Caesar was Dictator and High Priest, and had vanquished and subdued the nations that were most dangerous to Rome, and first of all men had begun to explore the unknown sea beyond the pillars of Hercules, and discovered the land of Britain, hitherto unknown to Rome; yet they slew him in the midst of what they call the sacred Senate-house, under the eyes of

---

[1] These "wrongs" would seem to be Antony's way of describing the resistance of the Senate to his attempt to make himself emperor by force of arms.

the Gods, defacing his body with twenty-three wounds, though they
had all been taken prisoners by him and spared, and though some
of their names were written in his will as his heirs. But the rest, instead of punishing the authors of this abomination, raised them to
office and honours, which they abused by seizing on public money [1]
for themselves, and levying an army against us. . . . Some of
them we have already punished; the rest with God's help you shall
shortly see chastised. We have already succeeded in the greatest
of our endeavours, and made subject to us Spain and Gaul, and the
districts nearer home. One task yet remains: to make war upon the
murderers of Caesar who are across the sea.[2] And since we intend to
conduct this war at a distance on your behalf, it does not seem to us
to be safe either for us, or for you, to leave the rest of our enemies
here behind us, since they would take advantage of our absence, and
lie in wait for the accidents of war. Nor do we think that, in the
present emergency, we ought to be slow to act from any consideration for them, but rather we must put them one and all out of the
way. We have no grudge against any large body of citizens, nor
shall we make [3] any choice of our private enemies nor shall we in the
least single out those who are wealthy or politically eminent, though
it must needs be that three men must have more enemies than one;
we shall not slay as many as did the last Dictator, whom you called
Sulla the Fortunate, although he too was called on to rule the city
during a civil war. And though we might arrest those whom we
know to be evil without warning, we prefer rather to proclaim their
names for your sakes, so that, having them properly named and
numbered, the soldiers may abstain from interfering with anyone
else. Therefore, with the blessing of heaven, we give command that
none shall harbour any of those whose names are written below.
Whosoever shall attempt to save them is included in the list. And
whosoever shall bring the head of any one of them to us, if he be a
free man, shall receive 2500 drachmae,[4] but if he be a slave he shall
receive 1000 drachmae, his freedom, and all the civic privileges of
his master. The same reward shall be given to anyone who shall
give information of their place of hiding. We shall not enter on
our records the names of any who earn these rewards.

---

[1] If there was any truth at all in this charge, it could relate only to provincial
revenues. Antony himself had left no public money in Rome for anyone else to
seize. It was, of course, Antony whose armies were unconstitutional; the senatorial
forces were legal enough.

[2] That is, Brutus and Cassius.

[3] This and the following clause would describe the principles on which the list was
made up with greater truth if the negatives were omitted.

[4] Roughly £100, though with a very much greater purchasing power than that
amount of money today.

Then followed the 2000 names of the victims.

Did ever murder speak so loud? The writing was doubtless that of Antony, but the signature is Octavian's, too. Yet within three years of this, Vergil published his Fourth Eclogue, a poet's dream of a new era of peace.[1]

Now hear the fate of the venerable patriot and orator Cicero, as related by Plutarch: [2]

At last he put himself in the hands of his servants, and ordered them to carry him by sea to Caieta, where he had a delightful retreat in the summer. There was a temple of Apollo on the coast, from which a flight of crows came, with great noise, toward Cicero's vessel, as it was making land. They perched on both sides the sailyard, where some sat croaking and others pecking at the ends of the ropes. All looked upon this as a bad omen; yet Cicero went on shore, and, entering his house, lay down to repose himself. On sight of this the servants began to reproach themselves. Then partly by entreaty, and partly by force, they got him into his litter, and carried him toward the sea.

Meanwhile the assassins came up. They were commanded by Herennius, a centurion, and Pompilius, a tribune, whom Cicero had formerly defended when under a prosecution. The doors of the house had been made fast, but they broke them open. Still Cicero did not appear, and the servants who were left behind said they knew nothing of him. But a young man, named Philologus, a freedman of his brother Quintus, whom Cicero had instructed in the liberal arts and sciences, informed the tribune that they were carrying the litter through a deep wood to the seaside. The tribune, taking a few soldiers with him, ran to the end of the walk where Cicero's party was to come out. But Cicero, perceiving that Herennius was approaching to meet him, ordered his servants to set the litter down [though a large number [3] of them had gathered and were preparing to defend him by force], and putting his left hand to his chin, as it was his custom to do, he looked steadfastly upon his murderers. Such an appearance of misery in his face, wasted with anxiety, so much affected the attendants of Herennius that they covered their faces. Cicero stretched his neck out of the litter to receive the blow, and Herennius slew him. Thus fell Cicero, in the sixty-fourth year of his age. Herennius cut off his head, and, by Antony's command, his hands too, with which he had written the Philippics [denouncing Antony's crimes].

---

[1] On this poem see Chapter 3, p. 50.
[2] Langhorne's translation, p. 614.   [3] This detail is from Appian.

When these parts of Cicero's body were brought to Rome, Antony happened to be holding an assembly for the election of magistrates. He ordered the head and hands to be fastened up over the Rostra, a dreadful spectacle to the Roman people, who thought they did not so much see the face of Cicero, as a picture of Antony's soul.

A glimpse of the outrage inflicted on altogether innocent people is given us by the story of a man called Restio. He had escaped with one slave, who had once been a favourite servant, but who had in some way misbehaved himself so that his master had branded him. Restio was startled to find that this slave had followed him, and expected that the slave would now avenge himself by turning informer. The slave, however, told him not to be alarmed, because he had not forgotten all the kindness he had received before he was branded, and so took his master to a cave and secretly supplied him with food for several days. Then as he found that several people in the place had begun to suspect his master's retreat, and found also that a body of soldiers was seeking for him, the slave ran after an old man whom he had noticed going alone along the road, cut off his head, brought it to the soldiers, and claimed the reward. The soldiers gave the slave nothing, but snatched away the head, so as to secure the reward for themselves, and hurried back to Rome. The slave then succeeded in getting his master safely off to sea.

The stupidity of the murderers appears very plainly in the proclamation of one of the triumvirs, Lepidus, who wished to celebrate a triumph for victories that he had won in Spain. Expecting, naturally enough, that people would be in no mood to engage in any public rejoicing, he put up this proclamation: "With the blessing of heaven, all good citizens, male and female, are to offer sacrifice, and observe this day as my festival, and anyone who is found not openly rejoicing shall be included in the list of the proscribed." He conducted his procession amid loud cheers.

And there are some absurdities of a less grim kind. A man called Pomponius, whose name was on the proscribed list, arrayed himself in his full uniform as a general, and dressing his slaves as lictors, marched through the streets of Rome with these men round him, and at the gates demanded public chariots to carry his party; thence he made his way through Italy, everyone giving him in terror what he wanted; finally he secured one of the ships of the navy to sail to Sextus Pompey, since he alleged that he had been sent to make peace with him on behalf of the Triumvirs.

Perhaps the most daring device which led to an escape was that of Ventidius, whom we hear of afterwards as a successful commander. He dressed himself up as a centurion, put himself at the head of a force of soldiers, and marched wherever he liked in Italy, searching for a man whose name was on the proscribed lists and whom, strangely enough, he could never find — the man he was searching for was himself!

Two examples of the devotion of slaves to their masters should not be omitted, though their names are not even known. A favourite slave of Appius, hearing that the soldiers were searching for his master, dressed himself up in his master's clothes and lay down on his master's couch, with his back to the light. The soldiers came and killed him, but the delay enabled his master to escape. And a man called Milennius escaped by the similar devotion of another slave, who dressed himself as his master, entered his master's sedan-chair, and persuaded his fellow slaves to carry him off in it and to break into a run just as the soldiers came into sight. They, seeing the litter being carried off, rushed after it and killed the faithful slave. But Milennius managed to escape.

Now turn to the story of Quintus Lucretius Vispullo himself, as Appian tells it.

Vispullo was wandering about the country with two good servants, but through lack of supplies was forced to turn homewards, riding in a litter as a sick man. But one of his bearers had injured his leg, so Vispullo had to walk, leaning on the other. As they came in sight of the gate [1] he saw a troop of soldiers running out; and, remembering that his father had been caught on that very spot in the Proscription of Sulla, he turned aside with one of his servants to hide in one of the

---

[1] Anyone who has been at Rome will remember how straight a course the Appian Way keeps for miles outside the gate.

tombs that stood beside the road. There they were safe until the evening, when they were visited by a party of tomb-robbers. But this faithful slave gave himself up to be stripped of all he had, to allow his master to escape. But Vispullo waited for him at the gate, and shared his clothes with him; so they safely reached his house in Rome, where his wife concealed him between the two parts of a double roof, until at last some friend succeeded in getting his name removed by Octavian from the list of the proscribed.

The identification of Vispullo with the author of the inscription has been worked out very carefully by Mommsen, whose commentary [1] on the chronological, historical, and legal points of the case left really nothing else for later scholars to add. But on the literary side of the inscription — in other words, of its interest as a record of human character and feeling — he has not a word to say. It was quite characteristic of the great Prussian to have no time for that. Not the least of the services rendered to letters by the late Dr. Warde Fowler was the chapter in his *Social Life at Rome* in which he dealt with the inscription from this point of view; and to this the reader may be referred for a discussion of many interesting details.

But a few paragraphs from the inscription itself, which was erected by Vispullo in memory of his wife when she died, must be quoted here if we wish to see the effect of the proscription on the nobler spirits in Rome. Vispullo and his wife, after his escape, had enjoyed many years of life together under the peaceful rule of the mature Augustus. The inscription is written in praise of the dead lady, but it differs in a characteristic way from other sepulchral eulogies in that it is addressed, not to the passer-by, or to the public, or to the family of the dead or to that of the speaker, but to the dead lady herself; so that it has an intimate tone, very unlike that of a funeral speech:

Such long union as we enjoyed, ended only by death, is rare, for we lived happily together for forty-one years, and you left me only wishing that the parting had come by my death and not by yours, as would, indeed, have been natural since I was the elder. I need

---

[1] See his notes in the *C. I. L.* at the places already cited.

not speak of all the good qualities which you shared with other true wives, your faithfulness, obedience, courtesy, and good humour; your assiduity in spinning and weaving, your religion without superstition, your inconspicuous dress and modest way of life, your affection for your own family, your kindness to your household, which you extended as much to my mother as to your own parents. But some qualities I must claim as having been peculiarly your own, and they are such as Fortune has made rare in human experience.

He then mentions various examples of her liberality and her administrative powers; and proceeds to describe how she had saved him on two separate occasions in the Civil War. The first appears to have been in 48 B.C., when Vispullo left Italy to join Pompey when he fled to Pharsalia; Vispullo was then put in command of Pompey's fleet in the Adriatic, which in vain attempted to prevent Caesar's crossing. On this occasion Turia gave him all her pearls and personal ornaments, and not only continued to send him fresh supplies from the estate, but defended the house, first against a troop of Julius Caesar's cavalry —until Caesar called them off; and then, a year later (47 B.C.), from what seems to have been a siege by Milo, who was then wandering about the south of Italy with a band of cut-throats. This incident is related on what survives of the fragment most recently discovered. Of his own later deliverance and his wife's share in it Vispullo writes thus:

I can hardly persuade myself to bring into the light of day our dearest and most treasured memories, by telling how I was saved by a sudden message which you sent me, warning me of pressing danger; you refused to let me make the rash attempt to escape from Italy, and persuaded me to adopt wiser counsels; you prepared for me a safe hiding-place, taking your sister and her husband into the secret, though thus they also took a share in my danger. I could not tell the whole story if I tried. It is enough to record that you saved me.[1] But I will confess that the bitterest experience I ever suffered was after my restoration had been granted by the generous decision of Augustus Caesar, at a time when he was absent from Rome. For then you boldly requested his colleague, Marcus Lepi-

---

[1] This reticence is interesting. Vispullo seems to have felt that the actual details of his concealment would be out of harmony with the dignified grace of this record, which was to be engraved on marble.

dus, who was in Rome, to carry out my restoration. But when you bowed before Lepidus, he not merely refused to lift you up, but ordered you to be dragged away and hustled and beaten like a slave. Your courage was not subdued and you forced him to recognise Caesar's edict, openly protesting against his insult, so that the world might know who had been the author of the danger in which I stood. And it was not long before he had reason to regret what he had done. . . . When peace was restored to the world and quiet government re-established, happy times fell to us too. We longed for children, which Fortune for a time had grudged us. And if only Fortune had continued the kindness which she began to show, we should have lacked no happiness; but her decree was otherwise.

Vispullo then passed to what seems to have struck him as one of the greatest of his wife's virtues, and we can at least realise the unselfishness of her attitude. From the phrase which follows we gather that they lost their only daughter soon after she was born; some years after that Turia made to her husband the proposal that he should divorce her in order to marry some wife who might bear him children, promising that she would treat the new wife like a sister and her children as if they were her own kin. Whatever we may think of this suggestion, Vispullo knew quite well what he thought:

I must confess that I was almost out of my mind to think that any divorce between us could be made except by death; that you should dream of ceasing to be my wife while you still lived, when you had been faithful to me all the years during which I had been almost a banished man. What desire or need had I of children that I should break my faith to you and sacrifice a certain for a doubtful happiness? I could not have yielded to such a suggestion without dishonour to myself and misery to us both.

He then relates how in accordance with Turia's own desire, he had adopted a daughter, and this is how the long inscription ends:

I might dwell on all your forethought and good counsel, but I must reserve this space rather for a tribute to your goodness, so that at least I may show how deeply I lament the wife whose memory I have sought to consecrate for ever. Do not think that your example will be forgotten, for your fair renown meets me at every turn and teaches me to be brave against ill fortune. Fate has not robbed me of everything, since it still suffers me to cherish the memory of your goodness, though I have lost all the peace of my soul in losing you. When I think how you were wont to foresee and provide against my dangers, I am broken down with the thought of my calamity, and I cannot be faithful to my promise not to grieve. Grief overcomes my resolution, and I am plunged in sorrow whether I look forward or backward; and the very greatness of your memory makes the rest of my life promise nothing but days of mourning. My last word shall be that there was nothing which your goodness did not deserve, but that I never succeeded in paying my debt. I have counted your last commands as a law, but I will spare no honour which they did not forbid me to render you. And now I pray that the unseen Powers with whom your spirit is, give you peace now and for ever.

II

WHERE WAS VERGIL'S FARM?[1]

In an earlier lecture, which dealt with the Youth of Vergil,[2] I followed the late Dr. Warde Fowler in trying to frame some picture of the circumstances under which Vergil's earliest poems were written and in which he was (or may have been) first brought into contact with the future ruler of the world, the young Octavian.[3] But no more than a passing reference was then possible to the old riddle of the precise locality in which Vergil's boyhood was spent. Of course we know that he was a citizen of Mantua; but the ancient Italian townships were all surrounded by a considerable area of land, and the farmers of this were all citizens of the particular town; and since, as we shall see, the nature of the country on different sides of Mantua is exceedingly different, it is not without interest to discover, if we can, in what particular point of the great sub-Alpine plain was placed the village (*pagus*) of Andes in which our ancient authorities tell us that Vergil was born. As long ago as 1915, my then colleague, Mr. (now Professor) G. E. K. Braunholtz, in the course of a long study of the ancient names of North Italy, had found definite evidence for identifying the village of Andes with a particular modern site.

[1] A large part of this chapter was first given as a lecture at the John Rylands Library on November 8, 1922. I have to thank my friends, Professors G. E. K. Braunholtz and W. M. Calder and Mr. Donald Atkinson, for much valuable help with the inscriptions; and my debt throughout to the wise and searching criticism of Professor W. B. Anderson is greater than I can easily express. Since 1922 I have twice re-visited the site and further explored the district with Count Lechi's kind help; and the text of the lecture has been thoroughly revised both before and since it was given at Harvard in March, 1927.

[2] *John Rylands Library Bulletin*, II (1915), 212; reprinted in *New Studies of a Great Inheritance*, 1921, p. 66.

[3] Dr. Warde Fowler supposed that Octavius was with his great-uncle Julius in Transpadane Gaul in the winter of 51–50 B.C. In three inscriptions of Brixia (*C. I. L.*, V, 4305–4307) I find welcome evidence, on Mommsen's almost certain showing, of a lively and continued interest which the princely youth took in that town in the years 44 and 43 B.C. and after. At some later date he made an aqueduct for them, which Tiberius renewed (*ibid.*, 4306).

1. The Mantuan district

Since then fortune[1] has allowed me to visit Mantua more than once, and to explore the sites concerned; and the object of this lecture is to explain the conditions of the literary and geographical problem and to submit further evidence in favour of Professor Braunholtz's view. The discovery itself must be ascribed to him.

One thing I will venture to assume — that is, that everyone is interested in Vergil; and even those who are more interested in poetry than in geography will perhaps be not unwilling to face a problem which bears upon the interpretation of a fascinating part of his poetry and a part frequently censured because its critics were wholly in the dark about this problem. If they have adopted any view at all, they have been content to take over from Dante a mediaeval tradition (pointing to Pietole) which is scarcely to be reconciled with evidence that we possess from sources almost contemporary with Vergil himself. And no one, I hope, will be unwilling to study a district which Vergil must have known exceedingly well and traversed scores of times in his schooldays when he studied first at Cremona and then at Milan — whether or not it contained the site of his father's farm. Here is a section of Kiepert's Map of North Italy, which shows the situation of the towns and rivers (Plate 1).

Recall now some of the difficulties which make the *Eclogues* of Vergil still full of dark places. So sane a critic as Professor Henry Nettleship [2] remarked that "the neighbourhood of

[1] Really, the liberal gift of the sabbatical furlough which the University of Manchester makes to its professors, and the sympathetic help of my friend Mrs. A. W. Benn of Florence, whose automobile rendered possible a visit to a great many points of the region between Mantua and Brescia within the limits of time to which I was bound at the beginning of June, 1922.

[2] *Ancient Lives of Vergil*, 1879, p. 49, where he alludes to a remark of Professor H. A. J. Munro. But in the *Journal of Philology*, VI (1876), 40, the passage which Nettleship no doubt had in mind, all that Munro says is this: "When I was at Tarentum a few months ago, it struck me how much better the scenery, flora, and silva of those parts suited many of the *Eclogues* than did the neighborhood of Mantua." The poem of Propertius, Book II (III), 34, which Munro was illustrating, alludes to Eclogues II, III, VII, IX, and (especially often) to X, to the *Georgics*, and to the coming *Aeneid*; and describes Vergil as singing of Thyrsis and Daphnis *umbrosi subter pineta Galaesi, i. e.*, at Tarentum. Munro suggests very happily that the *villula Sironis* (which Vergil and his father bought when expelled from their own [*Catalepton*, X]; cf. *Georg.*, IV, 125) may have been in that neighbourhood.

Mantua notoriously does not suit the description of scenery in the *Eclogues*." As it stands, this remark is about as illuminating as if one said that the description of scenery in Shakespeare's plays did not suit the neighbourhood of Stratford-on-Avon. The *Eclogues* are essentially dramatic; and to criticise their author because the scenery which he mentions appears to you different from the scenery of a particular part of a particular country is just as helpful as it would be to criticise Macbeth because he did not meet the witches on the banks of the Avon, or Hamlet because his father's ghost did not appear, say, on the battlements of Kenilworth Castle. It is obvious that we must enquire what is the background implied in each separate Eclogue before we can judge whether it is or is not consistent. In the Second Eclogue, for example, the speaker expressly declares that he has "a thousand sheep wandering on Sicilian mountains"; therefore they must be in Sicily; therefore it seems hardly worth while to complain that they are not in Mantua! Or take the Eighth Eclogue, which contains two separate poems: in the first the recurring refrain speaks of Arcadian song (*Maenalios versus*), and the whole atmosphere is Greek; in the second half, not merely the names but the whole subject is Theocritean, and the herbs used for the incantation come from Pontus; why should anyone want to discover Mantuan scenery in such a composition? The Tenth and Sixth Eclogues, as Skutsch [1] has shown, have no one scene: each of them follows Vergil's friend Gallus over the whole poetical world, taking small pictures, not to say snapshots, of his poetry, now in Arcadia, now in Thrace, now in Crete; as well as in that more shadowy region of the universe in which Pyrrha and Deucalion threw their stones. The Fourth Eclogue, as we know, is concerned with building a new world, with all the glories of every land newly set therein. Therefore, in five [2] out of the ten Eclogues the question of local scenery simply does not arise and it is merely darkening counsel to talk of it.

[1] *Aus Vergils Frühzeit*, chaps. 1 and 2, the results of which are briefly stated in *Great Inheritance*, pp. 68, 78 ff.

[2] That is, in Eclogues II, IV, VI, VIII, and X. It cannot be an accident that these are all even numbers. Vergil, in his silent way, has chosen from his early work five poems with a local setting, and five with a foreign setting, and arranged them alternately. On this feature in Vergil's method, see further Chapter 9, pp. 139 ff.

2. Mantua as it is

But what the critics, no doubt, do mean is this: that in the Eclogues where reference is definitely made to North Italian conditions—for instance, in the First—they have been unable to discover any features of scenery which they can identify with what they have seen in the neighbourhood of Mantua. How far they have explored the region of Mantua they do not say. The kind of territory which surrounds the city, *pascentem niueos herboso flumine cycnos*,[1] appears at once in the photograph (Plate 2); in the city itself, between the two lagoons, there could be no farm.

But what other Eclogues besides the First refer to Italian scenery? The Ninth, which also deals with Vergil's farm; the Seventh, whose scene is on the banks of the Mincius; and (less definitely) the Third and Fifth, in both of which one of the speakers is Menalcas, that is, Vergil, as we shall see. In the Third, Meliboeus and the Roman statesman Pollio are mentioned; in the Fifth, Menalcas claims the authorship of the Second and Third; and the Fifth is generally and rightly[2] regarded as a lament for Julius Caesar. But our chief concern must be with the First, Seventh, and Ninth, in which Rome and the Mincius, Mantua, and Cremona are all definitely named. The question is whether the neighbourhood of Mantua does or does not fit the details of the scenery in these five local Eclogues. If it does not, Vergil has made a sad mess. That is what his nineteenth-century critics took particular pleasure in supposing. What I shall now try to show, partly by means of typical photographs,[3] is that, although the indications of scenery which these poems contain do not harmonise with the traditional site of Andes, namely, the little village of Pietole about three miles southeast of Mantua, they do harmonise remarkably well with the site indicated by Professor Braunholtz.

[1] *Georg.*, II, 199.
[2] On this see now the penetrating and convincing study by Professor D. L. Drew in *Classical Quarterly*, XVI (1922), 57.
[3] Let me record my cordial gratitude to Professor Commendatore F. Carli, Secretary of the Chamber of Commerce of Brescia, who kindly arranged for procuring those of the Carpenedolo ridge; and even more to Count Teodoro Lechi, of Brescia and Calvisano, to whose generous and discriminating interest in the question I owe all the rest (save that of Pietole, which was taken by my wife in 1908).

First note briefly what information we have from sources outside Vergil's own writings. His biographers agree that the village of Andes was included in the township of Mantua; but only one of the ancient biographies, namely, that attributed to Probus, mentions its actual distance from that town. Of this biography Henry Nettleship writes: "This fragment, so far as it goes, is so good that we can only wish more had survived." [1] And he conjectures that it was "compiled independently from the same materials as those used by Suetonius." I see no reason whatever to doubt Nettleship's judgement; for the biography is one of the only two [2] that altogether exclude the element of fable, and the only one whose chronology, so far as it goes, is both precise and correct. It must therefore have been drawn from sources current in the first century of the Christian era; indeed, we may reasonably think that it was ultimately derived from the great scholar and critic, Valerius Probus, whose name it bears. Probus flourished under Nero and later, that is, from A.D. 56 to 88, and Nettleship writes that he is "inclined to assign to him without question the first place among commentators on Vergil." [3]

Now Probus tells us [4] that Andes was 30 miles from Mantua. That means, of course, 30 Roman miles, which is roughly equivalent to 45 kilometres, or 28 English miles. This appeared to Nettleship to be too far from Mantua to be true; but his only ground for the objection is that Mantua was a small city. So, however, were many other townships in Italy whose territory extended wider afield than 30 Roman miles; the hamlet of Hostilia, the modern Ostiglia, on the Po, 33 Roman miles from Verona, was nevertheless a *vicus* of Verona. [5] This was set out clearly in 1872 by Mommsen, [6] whom Nettleship [7] (in 1879) might have consulted before attacking the text

---

[1] *Ancient Lives of Vergil*, p. 31.
[2] Or three, if the curt record of his birth, death, and epitaph, which Diehl (*Vitae Vergilianae*, p. 45) labels "Filargyrius No. 2," be called a biography.
[3] See further Note B, p. 35, below.
[4] Diehl, *Vitae Verg.*, Bonn, 1911, p. 43; reprinted in Note B.
[5] See Tacitus, *Histories*, III, 9; Pliny, *Historia Naturalis*, XXI, 73.
[6] *C. I. L.*, V, 317.
[7] And still more Nissen in 1902 (*Italische Landeskunde*, II, 1, p. 204 n.).

of Probus on so flimsy a ground. Mommsen, who filled many interesting pages of the Corpus with the results of his special study of the confines of the Italian townships, found it impossible from the inscriptional evidence to determine precisely where the boundaries of Mantua ended[1] and those of Cremona, Verona, or Brixia began; but he entirely accepts the statement of Probus, and we are bound to do the same. On every critical ground it is improbable that so precise a statement on such a matter would be invented; other details given by the same authority, such as the age at which Vergil wrote the *Eclogues*, and the value of the property with which he was endowed by Augustus, seem to come from early sources and ultimately from Vergil himself. On this evidence alone Mommsen rejected the tradition which identified Andes with Pietole. Other grounds for the same rejection will soon appear.

What other evidence have we? Professor Braunholtz has drawn attention to two inscriptions containing the name of Vergil's father's family, the gens Vergilia, and that of his mother's, the gens Magia, respectively. There are only eight or nine occurrences of the name Vergilius or Vergilia among the many thousand ancient inscriptions from the whole of North Italy. Four of these are from townships remote from Mantua; three are from Verona, and one[2] is from Calvisano; a possible ninth occurrence we will consider shortly (p. 23).

The inscription from Calvisano is on a handsome altar and runs thus:

[1] See Mommsen on *C. I. L.*, V, 3827, and pp. 327, 406, 440. Observe also that in one of his sadly abridged accounts of the seizure (carried out by Octavius Musa) of the Mantuan lands, Servius Danielis (on Ecl. IX, 7) speaks of the process as extending "over fifteen miles of Mantuan territory." Unluckily it is far from clear whether this measurement is of the land confiscated, or of the land left to Mantua; or even in which direction it was taken: *usque ad eum autem locum perticam limitarem Octauius Musa porrexerat, limitator ab Augusto datus, id est, per XV. m. p. agri Mantuani.* Was Musa's limit a line drawn straight from Cremona to Mantua and somewhere touching the Vergilian property? or at right angles to this line? or merely, as *ad eum locum* should properly mean, from Cremona to the Vergilian farm itself, or at least to the point described in this line of the Eclogue (*qua se subducere colles incipiunt*)? In any case, as Professor W. B. Anderson points out to me, the statement definitely implies that the original territory was more than fifteen miles in breadth, in one direction at all events, and suggests that it was considerably broader.

[2] *C. I. L.*, V, 4137, now in the museum at Brescia, the ancient Brixia.

MATRONABUS
VERGILIA C. F. VERA
PRO MUNATIA T. F.
CATULLA V. S. L. M.

In the atmosphere of the Brescia Museum, where it is now, some of the face has unluckily crumbled; but when Mommsen saw it, it was complete except for the last *s* of the word *matronabus* and three letters in the word *Catulla*. The dedication is one of a common type, in which one woman pays a vow for the deliverance of another from danger. In a great number of cases the author of the vow is a mother, and the occasion is that her daughter is in her turn bearing a child. It seems probable that this was the case in the present instance because of the deities to whom the dedication is made. The *Matronae* were Keltic deities, whose name suggests that they would be worshipped by mothers.[1]

Let me remind you that in Roman nomenclature a married woman retains the Gentile name of her father. Thus the wife of Marcus Tullius Cicero was called Terentia because her father's name was Terentius; and Cicero's daughter before and after her marriage was called Tullia because her father was Marcus Tullius Cicero. Probably, then, this inscription was dedicated by a daughter of the Vergilian family who married into the Munatian family and whose daughter is therefore called Munatia. Now, when I add that Calvisano is exactly 30 Roman miles from Mantua, whereas Pietole is less than four, you have the first part of the case for Calvisano. This inscription of course does not prove that the Vergilii actually lived at Calvisano; nor can the Vergilia who made the vow have been a descendant of the poet, since he died unmarried; what it does prove is that some woman member of that family, probably after her marriage, lived near enough to Calvisano to make a votive offering there, probably for her daughter's safe

[1] Three other dedications to them appear from villages in the neighbourhood (*C. I. L.*, V, 4134, 4159, 4160), and two from Brixia (*ibid.*, 4246, 4247); of these, the first, like that from Calvisano, is dedicated for one woman's sake by another woman, her sister; one other by a woman, two by men, and one indeterminate. [Other Keltic cults, existing near Brixia, are mentioned by Nissen, *Ital. Landeskunde*, II, 1, p. 199. — W. B. A.]

delivery, and probably, if not certainly, in the first century of the Empire; for that is the period indicated by the style in which the letters of the inscription are cut. In an inscription [1] from Hasta (about 90 English miles to the west) two distinguished Vergilii appear within the same century, one of them a *praefectus Drusi Caesaris Germanici filii*.

But the altar from Calvisano is not all the evidence to which Professor Braunholtz appeals. Consider now another inscription [2] erected by a member of the gens of Vergil's mother,[3] namely, Publius Magius:

V   F

P. MAGIUS MANI

SIBI ET ASSELIAE M. F.

SABINAE UXORI

ET SATRIAE M. F.

TERTIAE

CASSIAE P. F. SECUNDAE

MATRI

That is to say: 'Publius Magius, the son of Manius, erected in his lifetime this tomb for himself and for his wife, Asselia Sabina, daughter of Marcus.' There is no doubt whatever about the meaning of the inscription so far; and these first four lines are all that bear directly upon the question we are discussing.[4]

Now, this inscription, which was put upon an elaborate and costly monument by a member of the family of Vergil's mother, Publius Magius, was found at a little place called Casalpoglio on the river Chiese, only 12 kilometres (7½ English miles) distant from Calvisano, and a little to the southwest of the direct road from Calvisano to Mantua. These two inscriptions do not, indeed, prove definitely that the branches of the Magian gens and the Vergilian gens which were allied to produce the poet were identical with the branches of these families which we find near Calvisano and at Casalpoglio; though the period to which both inscriptions belong,

---

[1] *C. I. L.*, V, 7567.   [2] *C. I. L.*, V, 4046.

[3] This name (*Magia*) is given by nearly all the ancient biographies, though in some of them (by a very common mediaeval corruption) it is spelt *Maia*.

[4] See Note D, p. 39, below.

to judge from the character of the lettering, is Vergil's own. That is, the inscriptions are cut in the style which marks the best work between 50 B.C. and A.D. 50, but which, from that epoch onwards, begins to be less usual. And if it was not these two branches that produced the poet, we have a threefold coincidence which is remarkable: (1) the finding traces of them in two villages so near to one another; (2) one of the villages being at exactly the distance from Mantua which Probus tells us was the distance of Vergil's farm from that same town; and (3) the inscriptions being both cut in the script of Vergil's epoch.

It is time to say something about the tradition which Dante [1] accepted, placing the site of Andes in the modern Pietole, two or three miles south-east of Mantua. So far as I can find, the origin of this tradition has not been traced; but on the strength of it a monument to Vergil was erected at Pietole not many years ago, which of course to every Italian eye is proof conclusive that that is the place where Vergil was born! In Mantua I fear that Professor Braunholtz and I are counted mere Bolsheviks, because we hold, in view of the evidence, that we are bound to do all we legally can to explode that handsome column.[2] Now, what was the origin of this belief

---

[1] In *Purgatorio*, XVIII, 83, Vergil is called

"quell' ombra gentil per cui si noma
Pietola più che villa Mantovana"

('that noble spirit for whose sake Pietola is more renowned than any other hamlet in the region of Mantua'). The interpretation of the last two words is that preferred by the best Italian scholars of my acquaintance in Italy and England, *e.g.*, my friend Professor Walter Ashburner, D.Litt., now of Oxford but long resident in Florence, who refers to *Patri Alleghierii Commentarium*, 1846, p. 425. Others take *villa* to mean *la città*, the town of Mantua itself. *Non nostrum est tantas componere lites.*

[2] One gentleman wrote to the local paper of Mantova, deploring the interference of wandering professors, tampering with every accepted tradition; and added that, since he had been Chairman of the Committee which erected the monument at Pietole, of course he must know the facts! Other local writers urge that, because Calvisano is not now included in Mantuan territory, it cannot have been so in Vergil's day. But the very act of confiscation by which Vergil was expelled was likely to sever the district from Mantua; and Count Lechi (in a letter of Sept. 9, 1927) points out to me that the attribution of places lying on the confines of two regions is not immutable; thus down to 1797 the townships of Castiglione and Asola belonged to Brescia, whereas they now belong to the diocese and province of Mantova.

Another Mantuan critic, Signor Balzo, thought that the fact that the *sepulchrum Bianoris* (*Ecl.*, IX, 60) could be seen half-way from Andes proved that Andes could

of Dante? I suggest that it lay in an inscription [1] which is now lost, but which the fifteenth-century scholar Jucundus says was on a stone 'beneath the altar of the [or a] large church at Pietole'; and slightly later another scholar, by name Pacedianus, said that he copied it when he stayed for some days at Mantua in 1517. Mommsen held it to be merely a forgery, but on what seem to be hardly sufficient grounds; and if this inscription, which contains the name of one P. Vergilius and which Jucundus says was found at Pietole, existed there in Dante's time, it would be very natural for people to take it as evidence for identifying Pietole with Andes. Jucundus gives it thus:

P. VERGILIO P. F.

PONT. MAX.

SABIN.

Even if Jucundus copied the text correctly, the stone must have been a mere fragment, for the last line contains part of a name which cannot belong to the person mentioned in the first line, because something else intervenes. Now Mommsen thought that the (supposed) forger based this inscription upon another,[2] which is said to have been found on the bank of the river Tartarus, near Verona. The nearest point of that river to Pietole is 12 miles away. Well, let us suppose that the would-be forger of the Pietole inscription traversed the 12 miles with his forging tools or, if he was content with a less literal kind of forging, that he sat in his study, sharpening his quill to increase the number of Latin inscriptions which he

not be at Calvisano. But he has reckoned without trigonometry: the distance at which an object is visible from a greater elevation is $\sqrt{2\,Rx + x^2}$, where R is the radius of the earth and x the elevation — which at Calvisano is 102 metres above Mantua. This gives us a distance of over thirty English miles, even without troubling to allow for any added fraction on account of the height of the tomb — if it existed and if it stood just outside Mantua; two assumptions which themselves are not beyond question. On a clear day, therefore, such a monument could be seen *all the way* — unless, indeed, we suppose that houses or trees intervened. Perhaps they did; but in that case the whole argumentation is worthless.

[1] *C. I. L.*, V, 3827 (*b*). [If the inscription, whether ancient or not, was actually in existence in Dante's time, it will afford an explanation of his belief. And if it actually existed, as Jucundus says, in the fifteenth century, it is not likely that it was a forgery but practically certain that it was ancient.—W. B. A.]

[2] *C. I. L.*, V, 3827 (*a*).

would boast of having 'found' — in either case, what had he to go upon? The Tartarus inscription as recorded by Cyriacus, a scholar who visited Verona in A.D. 1433 or 1434 and made a collection of its inscriptions, runs:

M. VERGILIO M. F.
ANTHIOCO VNIGENITO
SIBI ET PAMPHILO

Now, if the forger could invent the former of these inscriptions with nothing but the latter to go upon, we must credit him with a very vigorous imagination. The surprising *Pont. Max.*[1] of the second line is surely more likely to be either genuine, or a misreading, than a pure invention. And if the third line is what Jucundus had before him, it contains a detail which, to my mind, goes a long way to establish the genuineness of the inscription, because it is a detail which the would-be forger could not have arrived at for himself. The cognomen of the someone mentioned in this inscription of Jucundus, presumably the man who erected the monument, is, as you see, Sabinus. Now, we have just seen that a family whose cognomen was Sabinus was allied to the family which produced Vergil's mother, for Publius Magius (of Calvisano) had to wife Asselia Sabina.[2] It is therefore not in the least surprising to find that the Vergilian family which was allied with the Magian family also was associated with the Sabinus family. These three inscriptions taken together seem to me to make a strong case against mere coincidence and for the genuineness of the Pietole inscription. We need not therefore follow Mommsen in holding, as he did, that Jucundus or his informant forged it out of

---

[1] Caesar became Pontifex Maximus at Rome in 61 B.C., and after him Lepidus; afterwards the office was one of the emperor's prerogatives. That this should be the only record of its having been held before 61 B.C. by any member of the family into which Vergil was born would be a wildly improbable surmise. But there were Pontifices at Mantua (that they had some social standing is shown by *C. I. L.*, V, 4057, where they are named as recipients of a fine to be paid if certain property is misused), and the chief of them may have been called Pontifex Maximus. There is one other example of an Italian *municipium* with such an office, Vibo Valentia, in the extreme south (see Mommsen on *C. I. L.*, X, 49 and 50); and priests were probably numerous in a town so largely Etruscan as we know Mantua to have been (see, *e. g.*, Vergil, *Aen.*, X, 203: *Tusco de sanguine uires*). Hence the phrase in the inscription may be quite genuine.

[2] One Sextus Sabinus was Virgil's dearest school-fellow (*Catal.*, VII, 6).

nothing and that Pacedianus simply lied when he said that he had himself seen the inscription at Mantua. I am prepared, therefore, to believe that some member of the Vergilian family at some time was honoured at Pietole; but not that Pietole was the ancient Andes, the site of Vergil's own farm.

We have now seen what evidence there is outside Vergil's own writings for determining the question. But the most important part of our subject is the literary evidence from the Eclogues themselves; what kind of scenery should they lead us to look for?

As we have already seen, only five Eclogues can be called into evidence, namely, III, V, VII, and the two which concern Vergil's farm, I and IX. There are two points in the Third that may be regarded as indicating features in the scenery of the district. First, that a group of old beech trees (*ueteres fagos*, l. 12) seems to be mentioned as a well-known landmark, and is naturally identified with a similar group also mentioned as a landmark in the Ninth; and secondly, that the last line of this Third Eclogue,

<blockquote>claudite iam riuos, pueri; sat prata biberunt,</blockquote>

definitely places the scene in some region where irrigation of the fields regularly took place by means of opening and shutting sluices in the main water channels, to feed smaller rivulets running through the meadows.[1]

In the Fifth we have beech trees, hazels, elms, and repeated mention of an *antrum* or cave to which the two shepherds turn to find shelter from the heat;[2] cliffs (*rupes*), too, are mentioned, and the whole district is described as *montibus in nostris*.

---

[1] This aspect of the line was suggested to me by my friend the late Professor Charles E. Vaughan, when, in his last illness, I showed him, among the other photographs, that from which Plate 6 is taken.

[2] It is worth while to note that, though the mention of a cave was part of the pastoral scene in Theocritus, appearing in several Idylls, his ἄντρον is never what *antrum* always is in the *Eclogues*, a noon-day place of shade. It is the actual home of Polyphemus (XI, 44), of Cheiron (VII, 149), and of Menalcas (IX, 15), who boasts of its warmth in winter; and a secret haunt of lovers (III, 6). Of the serious use made of this Sicilian detail by Apollonius Rhodius and of its tragic adaptation in *Aen.*, IV, I have spoken elsewhere (*Great Inheritance*, p. 146). Since the word comes from Theocritus, we must not build too much on it in the *Eclogues*, but it does imply that the scenery included at least some hillside on which a shelter could be found from the sun, not a region of flat land, all meadows and swamps.

In the Seventh we find the river Mincius, and bees swarming in an oak tree. There is mention also of chestnut trees, which do not grow freely on the plain, and some reference to hills and mountains (ll. 56, 58) as normal parts of the scenery described by each of the shepherd poets in their competing quatrains. But this scenery is not necessarily connected with that implied by the mention of the Mincius in the prefatory passage.

We come to the kernel of the matter in the two Eclogues dealing with Vergil's farm, I and IX. In the First Eclogue, as we all remember, Meliboeus, who has been expelled from his farm, takes a sad leave of Tityrus, who has secured the continued possession of his by visiting Rome and obtaining a favourable response to his petition from some half-divine young ruler. This has been universally interpreted to mean that Vergil was threatened with expulsion, and then relieved from the danger by some promise given by Octavian.

But in the Ninth Eclogue [1] Menalcas is described as having addressed an appeal to Varus on behalf of Mantua, which was in danger through being too near to the luckless Cremona:

> Vare, tuum nomen, superet modo Mantua nobis,
> Mantua, uae, miserae nimium uicina Cremonae,
> cantantes sublime ferent ad sidera cycni.

Further, we learn that, although it had been said that Menalcas had saved his property by his poetry, nevertheless the report was untrue; the truth was that a stranger now held the property and that both Menalcas and his servant Moeris had barely escaped with their lives. The question whether this failure of the poet's appeal for protection preceded or followed the favourable answer of Octavian described in the first Eclogue (*pascite ut ante boues, pueri, submittite tauros*) has puzzled commentators from the earliest times. [2]

But it is not our concern here to determine in what particular month of 41 B.C. Vergil left the farm near Mantua which, beyond all doubt, had been his home for the first twenty-nine years of his life; what we want to discover is where that home precisely was.

---

[1] Lines 27-29.   [2] See Note A at the end of this lecture.

Let us turn, then, to the local descriptions which these two Eclogues give us. In the First there are three different pictures, two of which are fairly complete. The slightest of the three sketches is that of the scene in which the conversation of the Eclogue takes place. Meliboeus comes upon Tityrus while Tityrus is lying in the shade of a spreading beech tree; and when the conversation ends, Tityrus points to the tops of farmhouses in the distance, which, he says, were beginning to show their evening smoke; and points also to the 'lengthening shadows' of the 'high mountains.' Just now we saw that two of the other three local Eclogues speak of hills or mountains. We learn further that both of the shepherds lived near some small town, whither they used to take their lambs and cheese for sale.[1] The other two sketches are respectively of the farm in which Tityrus was going to stay [2] and of that which the less fortunate Meliboeus had to leave behind him.[3]

The farm that Meliboeus is leaving boasts of pears and vines and a green recess (*antrum*) [4] in which he could lie at length watching his sheep some distance off on a bushy slope, to which they seem to be 'hanging' by their feet, a description understood at once by anyone who has seen from a distance sheep browsing on a steep hillside. The same sheep, we learn, at other times fed on clover and the young willow shoots. That is the farm which Meliboeus had to leave; and it is clear that it is meant to include some stretch of hilly land. It is also clear that he was a near neighbour of Tityrus, who represents Vergil.

But what of the farm of Tityrus himself? This is described, in Vergil's way, in somewhat modest colours. It is 'big enough for you,' says Meliboeus, 'however much the grazing ground may be cumbered with bare stones or muddy reeds.' We learn

---

[1] Lines 22 and 35–36.
[2] Lines 49–59, 80–82.
[3] Lines 69, 75 ff.
[4] Mr. G. H. Hallam tells me that in 1923 he found "a cave of sorts, with a clay or sandy soil," at the eastern end of the highest part of the Carpenedolo ridge, about one third of a mile from the western end, just before the dip in the ridge where the cemetery is now placed. I had noted myself more than one recess, giving good shade with its steep grassy back and sides, though open at the top, in the eastern arm of the ridge, where it runs northwards.

further that it had a willow hedge beloved by the bees, a lofty
elm where the pigeons and turtle-doves cooed, and a cliff under
the shade of which the vine-dresser could rest and 'sing to the
breezes' (*hinc alta sub rupe canet frondator ad auras*).

We see then, from the mention of the bare stones and the
cliff, that this farm of Vergil is represented as containing at
least some portion of rocky country and some land bordering
on a reedy river. Other lines tell us of pine trees and more
than one stream; for Tityrus will enjoy the coolness of leafy
shadow among 'familiar rivers and sacred springs.'

What does the Ninth Eclogue add to the picture? Consider
the lines (7–10) describing the estate which Menalcas was
thought to have saved. These lines are quoted by Quintilian,
who tells us that they are literally true, except that Menalcas
means Vergil.[1]

> Certe equidem audieram qua se subducere colles
> incipiunt mollique iugum demittere cliuo
> usque ad aquam et ueteres, iam fracta cacumina, fagos,
> omnia carminibus uestrum seruasse Menalcan.

Here, then, is Vergil's own description of the land which he
could not save. It ran some distance — this is implied in the
words *omnia* and *usque* — from the point 'where the hills begin to withdraw and let their ridge sink by a gentle slope, right
down to the water and to the group of beeches, once tall trees,
now broken with age.' Here we have again the ancient beeches
which we noted in the Third Eclogue. It must have been a
spot which made some impression on Vergil's boyish mind,
partly, no doubt, because it marked the end of his father's
farm. We learn also that the trees stood somewhere near
water, though what water, we do not yet know.

Another point that appears clearly from this Eclogue is that
the farmers of Mantua were suffering because Mantua was too
near a neighbour to Cremona. This does not prove, but it certainly suggests, that the farms which Mantua was losing lay
on the side of Mantua nearest to Cremona. No one has ever
supposed that Mantua lost all its land. Moreover, when Vergil

---

[1] Quintilian, VIII, 6, 47; and so said Menalcas himself in Eclogue V, 86–87, when
he claimed the authorship of II and III.

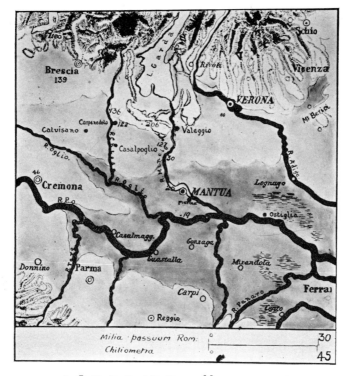

3. Orographic plan of the Mantuan district

Note. — *To the north of a line from Brescia to Vicenza the blackest parts denote the greatest Alpine heights; but south of that line (a) the light, (b) the darker, and (c) the darkest shading denote respectively an altitude above sea-level of (a) 200 metres and more, (b) between 200 and 25 metres, (c) less than 25 metres.*

4. Pietole

was looking back, in the little poem about the *villula Sironis*,[1] he speaks of it as having to replace for his father both Mantua and Cremona. Now, Pietole is about five kilometres southeast of Mantua, that is, on the far side from Cremona; but Calvisano is nearly equidistant from the two towns.

Now we may consider the actual topography of the district. Take first of all a map which gives a rough idea of the hilly and the marshy territory by marking the heights above sea level (Plate 3).

Mantua is only about 20 metres, or 66 feet, above the sea. It is almost surrounded by two large lagoons, and the whole district from there to the Po, the district in which Pietole lies, abounds in ditches and pools of practically stagnant water, because, as the map shows, the level of the water in the Po at the nearest point is 19 metres above sea level, so that there is hardly any fall at all between Mantua and the river, a distance of 14 kilometres (some nine English miles).

Plate 4 is a photograph of the so-called *fondo Virgilio* at Pietole. The country is bare and monotonous, level meadows shut off from stagnant pools by artificial dykes. In no direction are there any hills to be seen; both Alps and Apennines are far out of sight. If there were anything that could be called an *antrum* near Pietole, it could be only a sort of rat's hole, hollowed in some muddy bank of ditch or dyke. It is quite clear, therefore, that unless all the descriptions that we have followed in the local Eclogues are to be taken as mere inventions, Pietole cannot be identified with the ancient Andes; and it is difficult to suppose that the poet was merely romancing when he described, with a definite and practical purpose, the extent of his own farm.

But the land steadily rises the moment you pass northwestward from Mantua. In a mile or two you pass above the 25-metres level, and in a few more, above the 100-metres level, which means that you have been ascending all the way. By the time that you have reached Brescia you have passed the 200-metres level (660 feet), so that the ascent has been continued. The contrast is immediately perceptible as you travel,

---

[1] *Catalepton*, X; see further, p. 15, n. 2.

not merely in the clearness and freshness of the air, but to the
more trustworthy sense of vision, in the absence of swamps
and in the sudden life which appears in all the little streams,
often flowing by the side of the road. The water runs quickly
over bright pebbles, except where it is broken by a sluice holding it up into a pool in order to turn it into fields at the side,
just as we have seen described in Vergil's Third Eclogue.

Plates 5 and 6 are photographs of these roadside streams.
What of the hills? As we went northwest from Mantua
you may be sure that I kept a keen look-out for the first sight
of a hill. The first that appeared was a ridge, of which Plate 7
is a photograph.

This ridge, in the shape of the letter L, runs first roughly
from north to south, then turns toward the east. The tower in
the picture stands at its highest point, at the southeast corner.
This is the first hill of any description that you come to when
you go from Mantua toward Brescia. In other words, it is the
last outpost of the Alps northwest of Mantua. Nothing could
correspond more precisely to Vergil's description of the point
where the hills 'melt into the plain.' The little town at the
corner is called Carpenedolo.[1] The morainic ridge, as it runs
northward, forms for some miles the eastern watershed of the
river Chiese, whose channel is not far off, bringing down the
water from the Val Sabbia and the glaciers of the Adamello
group, which begins to rise to great heights some 25 English
miles north of Brescia. You will see from the map that at
Carpenedolo the road which lies at the foot of the hill has
reached a height of 122 metres, or over 400 feet, and rises
gently to 136 metres at Montechiari, the northern end of the
ridge.

Where is Calvisano? Just 8½ kilometres (5¼ English miles)
west of this; and from Calvisano the ridge with its tower is
easily seen — in fact, it bounds the landscape to the east. But
more than this. From Calvisano as you look north you see the
mass of the Alps. The snowy peaks are not visible except on

---

[1] The name means 'little group of hedgebeeches' (hornbeam, *carpinus*), and a
companion village a little farther northwest is called Castenedolo, 'little group of
chestnuts.' [There is a Carpenedo between Vicenza and Venice; and Carpineto
near Rome reflects the original form of the name. — W. B. A.]

5. Wayside stream near Carpenedolo

6. Wayside stream, with a small sluice, near Carpenedolo

clear days, but the hills in front of them, rising above 1600 feet immediately behind Brescia, which is some 15 English miles away, stand out and are regularly visible (see Plate 12, below).

One or two other photographs of the district may be added.

The bell tower of Calvisano (Plate 8) should be compared with the tower of Sant' Andrea of Mantua (Plate 9), which is slightly earlier. In several respects the two show the same type; if we disregard the lowest segment, which is concealed by the houses, we may say that each is divided into three sections by string-courses; each has its only window above the second string-course; in each an octagon surmounts the square tower; the octagon is crowned by a turret, conical at Mantua, spread into an ogee curve at Calvisano. But the towers of Cremona, Brescia, Verona, and Vicenza are markedly different, and the resemblance of the other two affords ground for believing that Calvisano maintained its connexion with Mantua right down to the Renaissance.

Just 13½ kilometres (8½ English miles) to the west is the river Mella (Plate 10), the only small river of North Italy which Vergil mentions in the *Georgics*.[1] It is named as the place where the shepherds pick a certain flower which serves as medicine for their sheep.

Vergil's farm, I take it, ran from some point of the Carpenedolo ridge down to the river Chiese, of which Plate 11 is a photograph, showing the Carpenedolo ridge behind it. The 'familiar streams' between which Tityrus could lie if he wished were either the Chiese and the Mella [2] or the Chiese and the Mincio, which cuts through the Carpenedolo ridge some 13 English miles farther to the east.[3]

Finally, let me add a photograph of the view northward from Calvisano, on which Count Lechi has spent a great deal of pains; it serves at least to show the outlines of the hills be-

[1] IV, 278.

[2] There is also a small intermediate rivulet, whose name, as I learn from Mr. Hallam, is the Naviglio.

[3] A small intermediate stream is marked on Kiepert's Map, but it must be very shallow, and dry in the summer in its upper course. In May, 1923, nothing broader than a ditch was to be found, in the latitude of Carpenedolo, between the Chiese and the Mincio.

hind Brescia. If you have had any experience of photographs taken from a distance of about 24 kilometres (15 English miles), you will not be surprised that their height is not imposing in the photograph. But their presence is an impressive feature of the landscape seen from Calvisano. Their dark grey sides tower up to a standing belt of clouds, which are torn into fantastic shapes by the winds scouring and buffeting the peaks behind. Only rarely the screen is broken, on some still day in winter or midsummer, and the great snowy heights themselves are seen. Could any landscape impress more deeply a young poet's mind? The rolling veil of cloud, always moving but never removed, always present but never the same, adds to the prospect an air of strangeness and mystery, that sense of an infinite unknown, which lovers of Vergil find to be the most characteristic thing in all his pictures of nature.

It is not much, you may say, to be able to identify a particular site with a particular ancient name; and yet in this case perhaps it is not altogether a waste of time, at least if we may hope that we have formed some picture of the lovely land which fed the imagination of Vergil when he was a child.

Additional Notes

A. *The Loss of Vergil's Farm*

The First Eclogue tells us that, while a multitude of unhappy people are being expelled from their lands round Cremona and Mantua, Vergil has received from a young ruler in Rome a promise that he shall not be disturbed. But from the Ninth Eclogue we learn that, although at one time it was believed that Vergil had been saved by his poetry, nevertheless he had been obliged to take to flight, and had been in risk of his life (*nec uiueret ipse Menalcas*), though a lucky warning enabled him to escape.

To these two perfectly definite statements the ancient commentaries and lives add a number of details, some probable and credible enough, — such as that Vergil's friends, Pollio and Gallus, had endeavoured to protect him, — others not easy to weave into a consistent story. In particular one authority, as we shall see, wished to date the events reflected by Eclogue IX as being *earlier* than those underlying Eclogue I; whereas others held that Eclogue I contained the beginning, and Eclogue IX the end, of the experience. *A priori*, the latter view is the simpler, since it accepts the order of the poems which the author has given to them; and in its favour is the broad and certain fact that before the Eclogues were published as a book, Vergil had ceased altogether to live in the north of Italy and never

7. The ridge of Carpenedolo

made his home there again. This conclusion we shall find to be entirely confirmed if we look into the evidence more closely.

The view quoted in the Servian Commentary [1] and by the Bernese Scholiast [2] is that, in spite of Octavian's ruling, Vergil was in the end expelled; and this view has been adopted by Professor E. Stampini, a recent editor of the *Eclogues*, as well as by Mommsen in *C. I. L.*, V, pp. 406 and 414, if I have understood him rightly. It is the natural implication of the two Eclogues as they stand, and it is supported by Martial (VIII, 56, 7–10), who tells us that, when Vergil had lost his farm and when Tityrus was mourning for his stolen sheep, Maecenas 'rescued him from poverty' — not that he restored him to his original farm. At the end of the *Georgics*, Vergil himself tells us that they were written near Naples; we have already seen (p. 15, n. 2) a possibility that before then he may have stayed for a time near Tarentum. The view of the Commentary (though not of the Life) attributed to Probus (Hagen, p. 328), that the events of Eclogue I are later in time than those of Eclogue IX, and that the poet deliberately mystified his readers for a courtly motive, is intrinsically improbable. There is nothing in any part of Vergil's work later than these two Eclogues to prove that at the time when it was written he was living in the north of Italy.

The Servian Commentary further implies (Servius Danielis, on Ecl. IX, 10, 11, 27, so also the Bernese Scholiast in his Preface to this Eclogue), that the change in Vergil's prospects was connected with the replacement of Pollio (*fugato Pollione*) as Governor of Cisalpine Gaul by Alfenus Varus. From the same authority (on Ecl. VI, 6) we learn (*a*) that Varus protected Vergil from a second expulsion; yet in his note on IX, 10, he states (*b*) that, thanks to the *iniquitas* of Varus, the Mantuans had nothing left to them but marshland (*nihil praeter palustria*), although he adds a quotation, from an orator whom he calls Cornelius, showing (*c*) that Varus had been commanded to leave them three miles of territory all round the walls.

From this Professor G. Thilo of Heidelberg, the late joint editor of Servius,[3] wished to infer that Vergil's estate lay within the three-mile limit, but (apart from the geographical absurdities discussed below in Note B) the assumption is gratuitous. If we argue, as Thilo does, that from the final description of the fate of the Mantuans, cooped up in their own lagoons, *the estate of Vergil was excepted*, though Servius does not say so, then there is no reason whatever why it should not have been equally excepted from the confiscatory enactment confining the territory of the town to three miles from its walls. If the statement (*b*) above requires modification by statement (*a*), so does statement (*c*), which is contained in the same note as statement (*b*).

Our trouble arises wholly from the lamentable process of repeated abridgement which all ancient commentaries have undergone in course of their transmission. We may note as an example that the high authority of

---

[1] Servius Danielis, on Ecl. IX, 11 (*non nulli*).
[2] Scholiasta Bernensis, Preface to Ecl. IX (*quidam*).
[3] *Fleckeisen's Jahrbuch*, XL (1894), 290, 302.

the extended version of the Servian Commentary (Servius Danielis) has been brilliantly established by Professor E. K. Rand in his paper on Donatus (*Class. Quart.*, X [1916], 158), where the reader will find evidence, incidentally, of the strange perversity of judgement which dogged Thilo's learning.

In this matter of the confiscation, restoration, and final loss of Vergil's farm, the successive abbreviators had an unusually trying problem. They had to deal, as practically all students of the question have agreed, with a series of events, any one of which might be briefly described in much the same terms as the rest, that is, that Octavian intervened in order to save Vergil, who was being expelled. Those who think with me that the authority of Probus is incomparably superior to every other (see Note B) will see that the first step was taken *post Mutinense bellum*, in 43 B.C.; in the restoration printed below to complete this sentence of Probus, I have conjectured that this first step was some promise to the soldiers (of lands in North Italy), to be carried out when Brutus and Cassius should have been finally defeated. From details given in the Lives we may safely infer that the fulfilment of this promise or purpose, so far as it would injure Vergil, was more than once hindered, with Octavian's sanction, and probably at Gallus's entreaty, first by Pollio and then by Varus. But the clamour and violence of the veterans, which Octavian was then powerless to resist, and which proved nearly fatal to Vergil's personal safety, in the end carried the day. All Octavian could do was to allow his wealthy supporter, Maecenas, to compensate Vergil for his terrible loss, immediately, no doubt, in hard cash, and before long by the gift of an estate in Campania. Among the stages of the loss the scattered fragments of the commentaries give us glimpses (*a*) of an appeal to Octavian; (*b*) of Pollio's protection; (*c*) of Octavius Musa's delimitation (see p. 19, n. 1); (*d*) of Octavian's new instructions (whatever they were) to Varus; (*e*) of Varus's final decision; (*f*) of a violent attack (or attacks) on Vergil's land by veterans discontented with the land granted (or seizing land not granted) to them. But so far as I can see, we have no means of knowing how far these events actually took place in this order, save that the first three preceded the second three: (*a*), (*b*), and (*c*) may have happened in any order, and so may (*d*), (*e*), and (*f*), save that (*d*) preceded (*e*) if the orator "Cornelius" spoke truth.

But from the uncertainties of these fragmentary comments we can, happily, appeal to Vergil himself. As Thilo saw (*op. cit.*, p. 302), the tone of the First Eclogue is mournful — indeed, bitter. The reference to the Civil Wars (ll. 71–72) is overt, and the soldiers are 'unnatural' and 'barbarous'; and though Meliboeus is surprised at Tityrus' fortune, he does not envy him (l. 11) for remaining in such a scene of turmoil and cruelty. But Thilo has not noticed, what is not less important, the complete difference of tone in Eclogue IX. Even where the confiscation is described, not civil strife (*discordia*), but merely ill luck (*fors*), is blamed; and the contrast is not between barbarians and peaceful cultivators (*barbarus has segetes*, l. 72) but merely between 'such poems as ours' (*nostra*) and 'weapons of war.' Moeris, the servant of Menalcas, is on speaking terms with the new *possessor*, and though he curses that possessor's kids, he is

8. THE BELL-TOWER OF CALVISANO

9. The bell-tower of S. Andrea, Mantua

taking them to market for him.[1] The entreaty to Varus which he quotes was no more than *superet modo Mantua nobis*, that the existence of Mantua should be secured — an entreaty which, in fact, was granted. And all the poems cited are from some time which seems long ago; some are half-forgotten. Since he wrote them, the poet seems to have "suffered a sea-change," as Shakespeare might have called it. And now, it is clear, there are many things in his mind besides the sad topic of the lost farm, which is mentioned for the last time in l. 29 — indeed, it would be truer to say in l. 16, since l. 29 only reports the prayer which has, in fact, saved Mantua from destruction. And in the remaining forty lines we find that the exiled Moeris is expected still (ll. 30–31) to keep bees and cows, and to rejoin his master soon (l. 67) and to hear more of his songs; so both he and Menalcas must be beyond any actual danger. Further, and most significantly, one of the poems recalls the great hopes of the new peace celebrated — clearly at an earlier date — in Eclogue V, recalling, indeed, even Eclogue IV.[2] And at the end, what are the last words, which to every Roman ear would give the omen and keynote of the whole poem? — *melius canemus* ('we shall sing better songs)'; whereas Eclogue I ends with the beautiful but grave prognostic of increasing gloom — *maioresque cadunt altis de montibus umbrae*. The shadows were very thick in the years 43, 42, and 41.

What, then, is Eclogue IX, and when was it written? Surely it is a typical case of the *praeteritorum malorum secura recordatio*. Eclogue X has been proved (see p. 16, above) to be a summary account of the poetry of Vergil's bosom friend, Gallus; is not the Eclogue that precedes it best regarded as containing something like a summary of Vergil's own past work, with specimens (*a*) of his purely rustic pastorals (23–25), (*b*) of his political appeal (27–29), (*c*) of his Theocritean romancing (39–43), and (*d*) of his prophecies of the new age (47–50)? Is there any topic in the preceding eight Eclogues which these four quotations do not represent — save the praises of Gallus in Eclogue VI? There was no need to allude to that poem; for it was more Gallus than Vergil, and Eclogue X was to take up that theme again. By the time Vergil wrote this Eclogue, and ended it with *melius canemus*, was he not already bidding good-bye to his early work and all its beloved surroundings, and reaching out to the vaster issues of the *Georgics* and the *Aeneid?*

B. *On the Life of Vergil attributed to Probus*

Nettleship's admiration for Probus (expressed in the fourth edition [1881] of Conington's *Virgil*, p. lxv) is based on the comments explicitly assigned to him by Gellius and others, not on the Commentary on the

---

[1] This seems to be the meaning of l. 6, *hos illi mittimus haedos*. It may mean, however, that Moeris was to meet the new proprietor in Mantua and hand over the kids to him there. It cannot mean that the farm was in the *urbs* (see p. 17).

[2] Compare IV, 5, with IX, 47; IV, 12 (*procedere*), with IX, 46 (*processit*); IV, 29 (*rubens uua*), with IX, 49 (*duceret uua colorem*); IV, 52 (*laetantur*), perhaps with IX, 48 (*gauderet*). But apart from these possible reminiscences, it will be readily admitted that the general tone of these five lines (IX, 46–50) is close to that of Eclogue IV — far closer than to that of the mournful Eclogue V.

Eclogues and *Georgics* which passes under his name but which contains matter in many respects dissimilar. In any case, the brief Life of Vergil stands on a different footing from the Commentary to which it is prefixed, and which has rather the appearance of a miscellany of Vergilian criticism drawn from several sources, some of which were exceedingly good and early, and some much later, as everyone admits. Nothing is more probable than that the compiler of such a handbook for teachers (perhaps in the fifth century A.D.) should introduce it by a short summary of Vergil's life, especially if he found one so good which bore the name of so high an authority as Valerius Probus of Berytus. No doubt the compiler abridged it in taking it over. And that so devoted a student and interpreter of Vergil as Probus is likely to have made some notes on his life can hardly be doubted.

The question which has been hotly debated for the last sixty years is whether the contents (so far as they go) of the actual document which we possess are worthy of Probus. It is so short, so interesting, and so little known, that I venture to reproduce it here. The text is that given by Diehl (*Vitae Verg.*, Bonn, 1911, p. 33), except that, in two places where the reading of the MSS differs (in the order of the words after *primumque* in the second sentence, and *cauisset* near the end), I have followed that of the edition of Egnatius (Venice, 1507); and that, in places where all editors admit that there is a lacuna in the text, I have inserted in italics the kind of restoration which to me appears possible. The reading *XXX* in the third line is that of the three existing MSS known to Hagen, and of the earliest edition (Rome, 1471; now at Florence, but known to me as yet only from Signor B. Nardi, *Sul Paese Natio di Virgilio*, Mantova, 1927). The edition of Egnatius reads (according to Signor Nardi), not *XXX* but *III*. The codex which Egnatius used appears to be lost; hence the value of the description of it (*antiquissimus*) which he ascribes to Merula must remain as doubtful as similar judgements of early humanists about some particular codex which had fallen into their hands. In any case, no scholar with any critical experience can hesitate as to which of the readings is more likely to be right, the *XXX* (of four known witnesses) or the *III* (of one, now lost); for no mediaeval scribe would think of changing *III* to *XXX* in such a statement; whereas only too many of them were likely to take the easy way out of the difficulty, which has been taken even by some modern editors, who ought to know better, and who have calmly tried to abolish the evidence which their ignorance of ancient Italy (see p. 18) made them unable to understand.

Vita Vergiliana Valerii Probi

P. Vergilius Maro natus Idibus Octobris Crasso et Pompeio consulibus matre Magia Polla patre Vergilio rustico uico Andico, qui abest a Mantua milia passuum XXX, tenui facultate nutritus. sed cum iam summis eloquentiae doctoribus uacaret, in belli ciuilis tempora incidit, quod Augustus aduersus Antonium gessit, primumque post Mutinense bellum <*ager eius in praemium uictoriae destinatus, deinde abreptus distributusque post Philippense bellum*> ueteranis, postea restitutus beneficio Alfeni Vari, Asinii Pollionis et Cornelii Galli, quibus in Bucolicis adulatur: deinde per gratiam Maecenatis in amicitiam Caesaris ductus est. uixit pluribus annis

10. THE RIVER MELLA

11. The river Chiese (Clesis), between Carpenedolo and Calvisano

liberali in otio, secutus Epicuri sectam, insigni concordia et familiaritate usus Quintili, Tuccae et Vari. scripsit Bucolica annos natus VIII et XX, Theocritum secutus, Georgica Hesiodum et Varronem. Aeneida ingressus bello Cantabrico, hanc quoque ingenti industria, <*ab Augusto ut opus maturaret appellatus, per reliquam uitam elaborabat*>. ab Augusto usque ad sestertium centies honestatus est. decessit in Calabria annum agens quinquagesimum et primum heredibus Augusto et Maecenate cum Proculo minore fratre. cuius sepulcro, quod est in uia Puteolana, hoc legitur epigramma:

> Mantua me genuit, Calabri rapuere, tenet nunc
> Parthenope: cecini pascua rura duces.

Aeneis seruata ab Augusto, quamuis ipse testamento cauisset, ne quid eorum, quae non edidisset, extaret [quod et Servius Varus hoc testatur epigrammate:

> iusserat haec rapidis aboleri carmina flammis
> Vergilius, Phrygium quae cecinere ducem.
> Tucca uetat Variusque; simul tu, maxime Caesar:
> non tibi, sed Latiae consulis historiae.]

Everyone admits that the portion in square brackets was added by the compiler.

This Life was criticised at length by Thilo,[1] who repeats and amplifies the objections raised in a Bonn dissertation by A. Riese in 1862. In 1906, E. Norden followed on the same side (*Rheinisches Museum*, LXI, 171) with an article in which there was nothing new save a rather surprising fierceness of tone, which suggests the impatience of one determined to be speedily quit of an unexpectedly complex theme — *improvisum aspris ueluti qui sentibus anguem pressit, humi nitens, trepidusque repente refugit.*

These criticisms, which I have studied with care, appear to me a mere tissue of guesses, involving assumptions possible only to persons who know nothing of the district of Mantua. Norden accepted a statement made to him privately by some unnamed acquaintance in Rome, that the scenery of Pietole harmonised well with the descriptions of Vergil's *Eclogues;* and Thilo calmly took for granted that within three Roman miles of Mantua there was some 'ridge of hills sinking into the plain'! Had the Universities of Heidelberg (in 1894) and Breslau (in 1906) no good maps of Northern Italy?

Apart from his own guesswork, the only criticisms which Thilo offers on the Life are concerned (1) with Keil's certainly inadequate restoration of the fragmentary sentence which refers to *Mutinense bellum*, on which restoration no more words need be wasted; (2) with the statement that Proculus was younger than Vergil, which, by combining ingeniously a string of notes from different sources, Thilo proves to be incompatible with a theory mentioned by Suetonius, that Eclogue V was a lament for the death of another brother, Flaccus. But that theory, which is quite unsupported and was never in the least credible, has been finally put out of court by Pro-

---

[1] *Fleckeisen's Jahrbuch*, XL (1894), 290–304.

fessor Drew's careful investigation (*Class. Quart.*, XVI [1922], 57) of that Eclogue. We know from Donatus that Valerius Proculus was Vergil's half-brother (*alio patre*)—a statement for which I find now welcome confirmation in an inscription of Verona (*C. I. L.*, V, 3409) on a tomb built by a lady named Magia Procula, the daughter of one C. Magius, who was a *Sevir Augustalis* of that town. The combination of the names vouches for an association between the families; there is nothing to prevent our supposing that this C. Magius (Proculus) was a cousin of Vergil's half-brother, though only by adoption, if, like most of the Augustales, he was a freedman.

(3) Thilo's third serious criticism is of the formation of the local adjective *Andicus*, which appears only in this Life, and which he supposes to betray "African Latin." On the contrary, it is excellent evidence, to any student of the ethnica of ancient Italy, that the biographer was using first-hand information; for this local suffix appears close by in *Arelica* (the ancient name of Peschiera), in the *pagus Farratic-(anus)* of *C. I. L.*, V, 4148, and in the villages *Betriacum, Erbuscum;* and it is characteristic alike of Liguria (as in *Ligusticus, Marici, Venascum*), of the Gauls (*Gallicus, Boicus, Avaricum*), and of the Veneti (*Veneticus, Carnicus; Benacus, Messanicus; Longaticum*). The form has been also vindicated by O. Brugmann (*Indogermanische Forschungen*, XXVI [1910], 128). On the ethnological significance of the suffix the curious may find full information in my article, *VOLSCI*, in the *Encyclopaedia Britannica* (11th edition). Lest any reader should be disturbed by the doubts of two such scholars as Thilo and Norden, let me add that the weight of authority is strongly against them. The excellence and early date of the material from which this Life has been drawn were recognised, not merely by Nettleship, but by three other eminent scholars who, like him, made a lifelong study of ancient commentaries —Jahn, Keil, and Ribbeck; and from a different point of view, and very emphatically, by Mommsen (*C. I. L.*, V, 406), whom Huelsen follows (in Pauly-Wissowa's *Realencyclopädie*, s.v. *Andes*). Martin Schanz (*Römische Literatur*, 3d edition, Munich, 1911, p. 32), though he gives more than enough room to Thilo's views, still puts the Life first in his list of Vergil biographies, calling it, quite truly, a "skeleton of facts." Some of these facts, as we have seen, are very interesting and not so precisely recorded, if recorded at all, by any other authority.

C. *Further Topographical Considerations*

After this lecture was delivered, Professor W. B. Anderson drew my attention to an interesting note of the veteran scholar, epigraphist, and explorer, Sir W. M. Ramsay, in Middleton and Mills's *Student's Companion to Latin Authors*, London, 1896, p. 148: "Virgil's farm was certainly not at Pietole, which is two miles south of Mantua on the flat plain; for (*a*) the farm was a long way from the city (*Ecl.* IX, 59); (*b*) it was beside hills (*ibid.*, 7 ff.); (*c*) woods were on or by it (cf. Donatus's [phrase of Vergil's father] *silvis coemendis* [and the reproach in Macrobius (V, 2, 1), *Veneto, inter siluas et frutices educto, rusticis parentibus nato*]); and the flat, fertile valley was certainly not abandoned to forests. After exploring the country, I felt clear that the farm was on the west bank of the Mincio, opposite Valeggio, where the northern hills sink to the dead level of the Po valley."

12. The Brescian Alps seen from Calvisano

Guided therefore by purely topographical considerations, without regard to the statement of Probus, and with no knowledge of the Calvisano inscription, Professor Ramsay determined on a site well to the north of Mantua and not very far (about 12 miles) east of Carpenedolo. This site would be far more credible than Pietole; but apart from the inscriptional evidence in favour of some spot nearer Calvisano and Casalpoglio, Valeggio is only 15 English miles from Mantua, and therefore not commended by the statement of Probus. Further, the narrow, romantic gorge of the river at Valeggio cannot be called a *mollis cliuus;* nor do the hills there 'sink into the plain,' for they continue some miles farther south, especially on the western bank. Vergil's farm stretched 'from where the hills begin to sink by a gentle slope right down to the water'; but at Valeggio the river has cut away the hill into a steep face and flows immediately below it. West of the Mincio there is no river until the Chiese is reached. After examining, in 1925, with Count Lechi, the whole stretch of the southward slopes between the two rivers, I am satisfied that the western end of the Carpenedolo ridge is the only district to which Vergil's descriptions can apply.

[Vergil's own description (*Georg.*, II, 198–202) of the confiscated land is worth noting:

> et qualem infelix amisit Mantua campum
> pascentem niueos herboso flumine cycnos.
> non liquidi gregibus fontes, non gramina derunt,
> et quantum longis carpent armenta diebus
> exigua tantum gelidus ros nocte reponet.

The *flumen* must be the Mincius, as Nissen says (*Ital. Landeskunde*, II, 1, p. 203); and I cannot help thinking that Vergil is referring to the Mincius valley north of Mantua; the small patch to the south seems hardly worthy of such magniloquent language. If I am right in this, Mantua must have lost a considerable stretch of territory to the north.—W. B. A.]

Let me add (1) that if, as seems most probable, the land taken from Mantua was contiguous with that taken from Cremona, Carpenedolo would lie just in the middle of this stretch from Cremona to the Mincio; and (2) that the *liquidi fontes* of l. 200 can hardly mean the stagnant ditches of Pietole.

D.   *On the second half of the P. Magius Inscription*

The second part is difficult. I was at first inclined to render it, 'who was also the mother of Satria T. (d. of M.) and Cassia Sec. (d. of P.),' taking the *et* after *uxori* as connecting that word with the final *matri* (just as in *C. I. L.*, V, 3710, a granddaughter, joining in an epitaph set up by her grandfather and uncles, pays her tribute *aviae et nutrici sue*), and supposing that Satria and Cassia were the daughters of Asselia by two previous husbands, and therefore step-daughters of P. Magius, no *et* being needed between their names, though it was felt to be wanted between those of other members of the family who were not in the same category. Parallels for this use and this omission of *et* in the same epitaph appear frequently, *e. g.*, from Verona in *C. I. L.*, V, 3440 (three wives and three sons but only one *et*, and that stands between the two groups), 3797, and 3822; from Cremona in *C. I. L.*, V, 4106. We may note that in V, 4073, a lady named Furia, from Mantua, erects a tomb for herself and her three husbands.

But Professor W. M. Calder, to whose friendly criticism I am greatly indebted, points out that by the practice regular in Latin epitaphs the word *matri* at the end, with the name immediately preceding it, ought to mean the mother of P. Magius himself, who is the author of the monument; and further, that the last person of the family group who is mentioned on such epitaphs is often added without any preceding *et*, as in *C. I. L.*, V, 4460 (from Brixia), where a man erects a tomb *sibi et . . . uxori et . . . fratri et . . . patri, Antoniae Catullae matri.* Two epitaphs from Verona (*ibid.*, 3673 and 3797) show exactly a parallel arrangement, save that the last person mentioned in the first was the author's *contubernalis*, in the second his *uxsor*. On the pattern of these inscriptions we should expect, if my first interpretation were correct, not *matri* but *privignis*.

These examples from the same neighbourhood carry great weight, but for the puzzling appearance of 'Satria Tertia the daughter of Marcus,' without any mention of her relation to Magius, between his wife and mother. Of this Professor Calder writes to me: "As this is a family tomb, Satria probably lived in the house of Magius and may have been a poor relation of his or his wife's. The occurrence of such names on sepulchral inscriptions, with no term of relationship attached, is common, and epigraphists are familiar with the confusion which they introduce into otherwise well-ordered *stemmata*."

We may note in passing that it is quite possible that Satria was homeless when P. Magius took her in, — many children were, in the generation after the Civil Wars, and the inscription may well be Augustan, — but improbable that she was poor; for from *C. I. L.*, V, 4049, from Medole, only a mile or two from Casalpoglio, we find that a Satria M. f. Tertia — who may well be the same person — was buried, not with Magius, but with P. Catius Callaui f. (presumably her husband) and other members of his family. And a few miles farther south, near Betriacum, on the line between Mantuan and Cremonese territory, a M. Satrius Maior in the second century erected a statue to Victory in honour of the two Emperors (Marcus Aurelius) Antoninus and Verus. The Satrian house was clearly one of some distinction.

But to return: I now regard Professor Calder's view of our inscription not merely as far the more probable, but as completely established, because I have found other examples of a person whose relation to the author of the inscription is not stated, being thus interpolated, in the list of his relatives, among the inscriptions of the district, *e. g.*, at Verona (*C. I. L.*, V, 3529 and 3742). The district is rich in family tombs.

My friend Mr. J. Peacock, of the John Rylands Library, reminds me of the famous epitaph in Salisbury Cathedral attributed to Ben Jonson, in which Mary Herbert, Countess of Pembroke, is described as "Sidney's sister, Pembroke's mother." But Salisbury is a long way from Calvisano. [This style can be paralleled on ancient *metrical* epitaphs; on a prose epitaph, especially a Latin one, such a deviation from the normal form would be made clearly, explicitly, and unmistakeably. — W. M. C.]

III

THE GOLDEN BOUGH [1]

No doubt we are all familiar with the Golden Bough which Aeneas had to find and carry off as his passport to the Underworld. And most of us who have any interest in primitive religion or folk-lore know the use which Sir James Frazer has made of the phrase as the title of his study of human superstitions, which, in all its three editions, he called *The Golden Bough*. But it is likely, even if we have from time to time quarried in the mines of learning, or strayed in the avenues of fancy to which that book, or, rather, those books, invite us, that we should find it hard to say just why he chose that name. And even if we did remember something about the Vegetable-Spirit, we might still find it difficult to recall how it was connected with Vergil's story of the descent of Aeneas. In truth, our difficulty is pardonable, since the question has worn more than one look to Sir James himself. In his first edition (1890) he took, or thought that he took, a theory from some anonymous ancient mythologist, connecting Vergil's golden branch with the weird custom of the runaway priest or 'king' (*rex nemorensis*) of Diana's grove at Nemi, near Aricia, some twenty-five miles from Rome. Hear how Sir James Frazer described it in his opening chapter:

In antiquity this sylvan landscape was the scene of a strange and recurring tragedy. On the northern [2] shore of the lake, right under the precipitous cliffs on which the modern village of Nemi is perched, stood the sacred grove and sanctuary of Diana Nemorensis. . . . In this sacred grove there grew a certain tree, round which at any time of the day, and probably far into the night, a strange figure might be seen to prowl. In his hand he carried a drawn sword, and he kept peering warily about him as if every in-

[1] This lecture, based on a brief paper which I published in *Discovery* (May, 1922), was delivered at Harvard in April, 1927.
[2] So Sir James wrote; but when I was at Nemi in 1926 the precipitous cliff stood where Baedeker's map shows it, to the east of the lake.

stant he expected to be set upon by an enemy. He was a priest and a murderer; and the man for whom he looked was sooner or later to murder him and hold the priesthood in his stead. Such was the rule of the sanctuary. A candidate for the priesthood could only succeed to office by slaying the priest, and having slain him, he held office till he was himself slain by a stronger.

The cult of the Arician grove [Sir James added][1] was essentially that of a tree-spirit. The King of the Wood could only be assailed by him who had plucked the Golden Bough. His life was bound up with that of the tree . . . and was safe from assault so long as the bough or the tree remained uninjured.

He then explained that the vegetable god incarnate had to be sacrificed as soon as another candidate for godship who could boast a larger portion of vegetable spirit, that is, of physical strength, showed himself in the neighbourhood. Of Aeneas' bough he wrote:[2] "Tradition averred that the fateful branch was that golden bough which Aeneas plucked before he essayed his perilous journey."

Of all the words that are overworked in a stammering world, there is probably no one word which can claim our pity more than the innocent verb "to be." You observe that Sir James said that, according to tradition, the branch broken at Nemi *was* the golden bough which Aeneas plucked. Well, as we shall see, this word "was" conceals many possibilities. But Sir James did not regard himself as responsible for the statement, but professed to be quoting it from a note of the old Vergilian commentator, Servius.[3] Now, in fact, Servius begins by saying that some people gave the bough a mystic meaning connected with the worship of Proserpine; and then goes on to add, as a further explanation (or illustration), what he says was a *publica opinio*,[4] that is, "a common notion," the story of the custom at Nemi. Servius then remarks that from this custom Vergil took the suggestion (*istum colorem sumpsit*), and adds that it was appropriate that the bough should be plucked because of the death of Misenus which follows. The breaking of

---

[1] *The Golden Bough*, I, 107.   [2] *Ibid.*, p. 4.
[3] On *Aeneid*, VI, 136.
[4] Sir James Frazer's rendering of this as "Italian tradition" (1st ed., I, 364 n.), and "general opinion" ("Balder the Beautiful," II, 284 n.) ought hardly to satisfy a Latin scholar. And the word *color* he altogether disregards.

the bough and its connexion with death are the points which Servius has in mind. This is a very different thing from saying that the bough which Aeneas plucked "was" the bough which was plucked at Nemi. To Servius the whole thing is merely a *color*, — that is, a suggestion, — and he would have been astounded if he had been told that on his authority, some fifteen centuries after his day, Aeneas was going to be identified with the murderous runaway slave of Nemi. All that Vergil did was to take the picture of a bough that had to be broken in a forest, and use it for his own purpose, which is obviously quite different. But indeed we need hardly trouble to criticise for ourselves Sir James's first handling of Vergil's story, for no criticism that any of us would venture to offer could possibly be as severe as the treatment which Sir James Frazer himself gives to his earlier theory, in the later editions of his book. In his *Early History of the Kingship* [1] he explained the runaway slave, not so much as a vegetable god, but as an incarnate Jupiter, a survival of the religious side of the kingship of some tribe whose name, alas, is not recorded, but who, for some reason or other, — also not recorded, — dumped their King-Spiritual into the somewhat depressing surroundings of Diana's temple at Nemi, just twenty-five miles from Rome, with no one to see that the rules of his sacred game were kept, and then went off to some region, also not recorded, — certainly not Rome, — with their King-Secular to conduct their public business for them, without having to worry himself any further about mistletoe boughs and godships and murderous rivals.

And in 1913, in the preface to the part of the third edition which he calls "Balder the Beautiful," Sir James writes as follows:

In this concluding part of "The Golden Bough," I have discussed the problem which gives its title to the whole work. If I am right, the Golden Bough over which the King of the Wood, Diana's priest at Aricia, kept watch and ward was no other than a branch of mistletoe . . . and as the plucking of the bough was a necessary prelude to the slaughter of the priest, I have been led to institute

[1] London, 1905, p. 203.

a parallel between the King of the Wood at Nemi and the Norse god Balder, who was worshipped in a sacred grove . . . and was said to have perished by a stroke of mistletoe, which alone of all things on earth or in heaven could wound him. . . . Though I am now less than ever disposed to lay weight on the analogy between the Italian priest and the Norse god, I have allowed it [presumably the title of the book is meant] to stand because it furnishes me with a pretext for discussing not only the general question of the external soul in popular superstition, but also the fire-festivals of Europe. . . . Thus Balder the Beautiful in my hands is little more than a stalking-horse to carry two heavy pack-loads of facts. And what is true of Balder applies equally to the priest of Nemi himself, the nominal hero of the long tragedy of human folly and suffering which has unrolled itself before the readers of these volumes and on which the curtain is now about to fall. He, too . . . is merely a puppet, and it is time to unmask him before laying him up in the box.

[And he adds on p. x:] This change of view affects my interpretation of the priest of Diana at Aricia, if I may take that discarded puppet out of the box again for a moment. Jupiter's priest cannot have been a mere incarnation of the sacred oak.

Sir James then turns to his new theory that the mistletoe bough was regarded as a "smouldering thunderbolt," a piece of lightning which had dropped from the sky; and we are now bidden to think that Aeneas plucked it as a kind of living torch, "a lamp to his feet as well as a staff to his hands." [1] On this, one must at least remark that Aeneas never dreamt of using as a staff so frail and slender a growth; and if it was a torch, it is a pity that he had to leave it behind him at Queen Proserpine's palace, at the outset of his journey through the region of darkness. And, quite apart from Aeneas, less imaginative persons than Sir James Frazer cannot but ask whether a primitive savage would be likely to identify with lightning, or even with a torch, the limp and sickly yellow stalks and the dull, white, viscous berries in which the mistletoe maintains its parasitic life.

Even this brief survey of Sir James Frazer's efforts must, I think, convince any reasonable mind that the resources of anthropology have given us no help here. Nor would it have been worth while to spend even so much time upon it but for

[1] *Balder the Beautiful*, II, 294.

the fame of Sir James Frazer's book and the respect due to so great a scholar, so learned a student of folk-lore, whose guidance in this case we must respectfully decline.

The result is that poor Aeneas is left in a mist. All we know is that he plucked a golden bough, that he carried it with him to the Underworld, and that he fixed it on the door of the infernal palace of Queen Proserpine, the bride of "dusky Dis." Why he should have done so, not even the most learned of commentators on the Sixth Book, the great Berlin scholar Eduard Norden, attempts to explain, save by the conjecture that Vergil must be following some piece of folk-lore unknown to us.[1] Is there, I wonder, any other incident, in the whole range of ancient story, so fascinating and romantic, so arresting even to a child's imagination, whose source is so wholly unknown?

Now, there is one avenue of interpretation which has not been tried, yet which to some of us is the most important of all, even though it may not be very satisfying to those who study anthropology for its own sake. I mean the question whether in Vergil's own poem there are any indications of the kind of ideas with which this picturesque detail was linked in his mind — whether, in other words, Vergil had, even in part, or at times, any thought of an allegorical meaning beyond the plain value of the bough as helping the movement of the story; and, if so, what that allegorical notion may have been.

No one can be confident that Vergil would be willing to answer such questions if we could put them to him. He might tell us to read the story for ourselves; and add that we were welcome to profit by anything we found in it, but that he could not put his story into prose, not even the prose of philosophy, because that would destroy it. He might even ask us, in our turn, whether we did not like the Golden Bough where Aeneas plucked it, and where Aeneas left it; whether we did

---

[1] Sir William Ridgeway's suggestion (*Dramas and Dramatic Dances*, 1915, p. 17) is not in itself incredible: that Vergil's ilex was connected in his mind with the trees regarded as sacred because they had grown over a tomb (*cf. Aen.*, III, 22), and so were linked with the Underworld. Professor H. W. Prescott (*Development of Vergil's Art*, 1927, p. 171) points out that in the older *Edda* Loki uses a branch of mistletoe before which the gates of hell open. If this is not derived from Vergil's story, it is an interesting parallel; but who can be sure that it is not so derived?

not think that it was in place in either case; whether we thought there could have been such a story without it. All this, Master Vergil, as Roger Ascham no doubt called him, might fairly ask us, and we could answer each question in only one way.

Nevertheless, readers of poetry, though they may not want the poetry altered by a single scene or word, have, after all, a right to try to translate it into their own humble prose; and, indeed, if they do not attempt such a translation, they can never be sure that they have reached the meaning which it really carries. A poet may and must put his suggestions into pictures. But his readers will always ask what the picture means. And if we find that a particular image in any one poet is closely associated with a certain train of thought, then at least we may be sure that there is nothing in the image which is inconsistent with the thought; and we may guess, though we cannot be sure, that that thought itself is some part of what the image was intended to suggest.

So our enquiry now will not be a matter of folk-lore, — not what the ancient Italian peasants believed about the mistle-toe, nor why they believed it, interesting as such questions may be, — but rather this: what ideas does Vergil connect most closely with this golden image?

It was essential to the purpose of Aeneas — that much everyone sees. It carried him through the Underworld in safety; it kept him living in a region where all else was dead; it reduced the "grim ferryman," Charon, to obedience; it made even the ruling powers of the dead world complaisant. Is it not, then, well to ask what else is essential to the errand of Aeneas? What commands are given him? What kind of motive is enjoined upon him? What kind of meeting does he seek, or find? What kind of revelation crowns his journey?

Consider first into what class of persons Aeneas was admitted by gathering the bough. The Sibyl tells us (l. 129): a few whom just Jove has loved, or whose fiery prowess has lifted them to Heaven, themselves of divine birth — only these have been allowed to enter and leave the Underworld alive. Clearly, therefore, there is something divine about the

Bough, some element of power that reaches beyond mortality. Can we discover in what this divine character consists?

What is Aeneas sent to do? Nothing in itself transcendent, not to rescue a bride, or to make any change in the gloomy region he enters. No, he is only going to see his father. True, he is to receive from him a revelation. But the revelation has partly been given. He knows already that he is to found a new nation, and a great nation; and he has actually reached Italy, which is to be that nation's home. What he has to learn is mainly the importance to mankind of the work which that nation will do; in particular, the restoration of the Golden Age, to be accomplished by the great Augustus. For in his reign peace was to return to an afflicted world; justice, free intercourse, harmony, and merciful government were to be everywhere established. That is the climax of the revelation. But at the moment when Aeneas is seeking the Bough he has in his mind nothing but the longing to see his father; and when he arrives, his father greets him, knowing nothing of the Bough, but seeing the cause of his son's triumph over the powers of darkness only in that son's affection. So that, whereas the Sibyl might have said, "It is the Golden Bough that has brought you here," Anchises does actually say, 'It is your own *pietas*, your own devoted affection, which I knew would not disappoint me.'

This double description of the power which brought Aeneas on his way is most characteristic of Vergil:[1] first, the supernatural image linked with some lost chapter of folk-lore; and, second, the natural motive which Anchises — who, after all, saw things from a loftier point of view than the Sibyl — recognises as the moving cause of the journey.

But again, how did Aeneas come to find the Bough? Only because he delayed his departure from the upper world in order to render the last honour he could to a friend who had been suddenly cut off; and to render it by hard work, felling trunks of trees to build a lofty pyre, and penetrating into the heart of the wood to seek them. The Golden Bough, then, would seem

---

[1] On this feature in Vergil's thought see p. 100, below.

to grow somewhere beside the path which men tread who do honour to their friends at a cost to themselves.

And when does Aeneas find it? The discovery is granted in direct answer to a prayer. That, of course, is not strange, seeing what divine power the Bough has when once discovered. Yet it adds a point to its character. It is divine, we knew. But we know now that it is given to those — and presumably only to those — who approach its divine creators and sponsors in the attitude of reverence and of what in our own phraseology might be called faith.

Yet again, how are the eyes of Aeneas actually guided to the Bough? By two twin doves whom he recognises as sacred to his mother, Venus; they fly before him into the forest just far enough to lead him on without passing out of his sight; and they finally settle on the tree 'whence through the boughs flashed the strange, half-breathing gleam of gold' (*discolor unde auri per ramos aura refulsit*).

Now, in the *Aeneid* Venus is, no doubt, a mixed character. She often does great harm. But so far as Aeneas is concerned, she is always trying — in her own too clever ways — to do what a mother should; and in his relation to her there is never anything but reverence and affection, which indeed are expressed in his words at the point when he sees the doves. And the doves themselves are connected with the better side of the activities of Venus. They suggest, not the storm and stress of passion, but the calm of steady and settled affection, the light and warmth of home.

The point need not, surely, be laboured further. If the Golden Bough was not connected in Vergil's mind with the strength of natural affection, with the ties between father and son, between son and mother, between friend and friend, then it was at least a most happy accident that, in his story, linked such motives so closely to so beautiful an image. And in great poets accidents rarely happen.

Without some specific declaration from the poet himself, such as good John Bunyan loved to prefix, and infix, and superfix to every part of his allegories, or such as even Spenser and Milton did not, at times, disdain to add to their own stately pictures — without some such confession on the poet's part, we are bound to limit our conjectures by a prudent "perhaps." Yet one thing at least about Vergil is not a "perhaps," but certain and demonstrable — namely, that to him a great part of the interest of nature and of humanity lay in the ties of affection which he found running through the mysterious fabric of both, linking the parts of each together and both into one not less surely than any physical law.

Of the effects of this habit of mind in the *Aeneid* more will be said in a subsequent lecture;[1] here let me illustrate it from Vergil's earlier work.

There is now a general agreement among Vergilian scholars, including the late Dr. Warde Fowler, Professor E. K. Rand, and Professor D. L. Drew, that the evidence external and internal for Vergil's authorship of the *Culex* is too strong to be doubted. Donatus tells us that Vergil wrote this poem when he was a schoolboy of sixteen; and it is certainly a juvenile performance. Some mention of it is natural here, because it contains Vergil's first study of the traditions which he found in books and in popular belief about the life after death; the central part of the poem is a picture of the Underworld which in many details foreshadows, in a childish kind of way, the great vision of the Sixth Book of the *Aeneid*. But we are now concerned only with one aspect of this poem, and that is the framework of the story in which the picture is set. How did the boy poet connect the Underworld with any story about a gnat? In an exceedingly simple and artless fashion. A shepherd falls asleep, and is on the point of being killed by a poisonous snake. His danger is seen by a gnat, who is filled with pity, and wakes him by her sting. This saves the shepherd, but is fatal to the gnat herself, whom he kills in the moment of his waking, before he kills the snake. But in the following night he has a dream, in which he is visited by the ghost of the gnat, who, reproaching him (gently) for having killed her, tells him of her experience in the world of the dead, — indeed, she lectures to him eloquently for 150 lines, — and then departs, not, please observe, with the curses proper to a ghost visiting

[1] See Chapter 7.

its murderer, but with a blessing: 'I depart never to see thee more; but do thou dwell happy beside thy stream and the green forest land and the pastures.'[1] When the shepherd wakes, he is struck with remorse and builds a tomb of earth and sods of turf in honour of the gnat, plants on it a multitude of flowers, and inscribes a tablet to say that he offers this honour to the gnat in gratitude for her having saved his life. So the poem ends in a garden of colour and fragrance, representing the gratitude paid by a human member of creation to a tiny non-human creature who had sacrificed herself for his sake. The likeness of this to the interest and sympathy with which Vergil always speaks of small creatures in the *Georgics* is obvious; and it is worth while observing how unmistakeable, even in this childish story, are the notes of forgiveness, gratitude, and goodwill.

Turn now to a more famous poem, the Fourth Eclogue. I must beg you to take for granted the answer now given by almost all responsible scholars to the fascinating historical problem[2] which it presents. Written in the year 40 B.C., at a moment when the Civil Wars seemed to be coming to an end because of the reconciliation between Octavian and Mark Antony, it heralds also the expected birth of an heir to Octavian. This child proved to be a girl, much to Octavian's disappointment. But to celebrate the approaching birth Vergil embodied in a shepherd's prophecy his hopes for a new era, a golden age of peace, in which regenerate humanity should enjoy every kind of blessing.

In the lines quoted below (with a few changes) from the version of the poem which I attempted in 1907,[3] I beg that you will note how the characteristic which we have been tracing so far is really the animating spirit of the poem.

The likenesses between Vergil's prophecy and the Messianic visions of the Hebrew prophets, especially those attrib-

---

[1] 'digredior nunquam rediturus: tu cole fontem
　　et uirides nemorum saltus et pascua laetus' (*Culex*, l. 381).
[2] See *The Messianic Eclogue of Virgil* (Mayor, Fowler, and Conway, 1907); the Old Testament parallels are treated more fully in *Virgil and Isaiah* (T. F. Royds, 1917).
[3] As an introduction to the joint discussion of Eclogue IV just cited.

uted to Isaiah,[1] have long ago been pointed out; and it is
generally agreed that Vergil must have had, directly or in-
directly, some acquaintance with these oriental hopes. We all
remember how Isaiah connects his golden age in the future
with the birth of a child, who is to be a king reigning in right-
eousness, restoring the innocence of the world, bringing peace
between all creatures and between men, so that serpents shall
not be poisonous and wild beasts shall become fit company
for little children, and the whole world shall rejoice. All these
features appear in Vergil's picture, too. But there is one
thing that Isaiah's conception of the Messiah's duty includes
which does not appear in Vergil, namely, his "slaying the
wicked." [2] By the time Vergil's infant has grown to manhood
all the world will be at peace (*pacatus*). And I do not think
anyone has pointed out how much there is in the poem which,
so far as we can yet tell, is peculiar to Vergil himself, and
remains so even if we have studied the great collection of
Messianic beliefs which Eduard Norden has recently made.[3]
Naturally enough, in all these the child to come has something
of an abstract character. He is to realise some political or religious aspirations; and it is these aspirations rather than anything proper to an ordinary child which fill that interesting
volume of human thought.

Now notice the difference in Vergil. In the first Eclogue, as
Dr. Mackail has pointed out, the lines of simple pity for the
mother sheep who stumbles and whose young are born dead
struck a strangely new note of direct natural feeling in the
conventional music of the Pastoral—music, that is, which was
attributed to the Sicilian shepherds, in the Alexandrian school
of poetry. The shepherd's Muse was for once uttering the
thoughts of one who was himself familiar with keeping sheep.
Just so, here in the Fourth Eclogue Vergil cannot think of the
birth of a child without unconsciously dwelling on the simple
human aspects of such an event. He addresses, not his nation,
or its ruler, but the child itself; twice he calls it 'little,' and
once, 'dear.' The earth is to provide the child with play-

---

[1] Chaps. I, X, and XI.   [2] Isaiah, XI, 4.
[3] *Die Geburt des Kindes*, 1924.

things (*munuscula*). The blossoms that grow around the
baby's cradle will 'caress' its face (*blandos tibi flores*). The
same playful tone appears in the picture of other living creatures; for the she-goats are to come home, unsummoned, to
bring their milk; the sheep will grow with fleeces of different
hues, so that no dye will be needed to make them into pretty
garments; the colours for the child's dress, saffron, scarlet, or
crimson, are to be there already. And the smile with which the
baby is to greet its mother is not less natural because Vergil
knew, as I have no doubt he did, what Pliny tells us,[1] that
Zoroaster, the great Persian sage, was said to have smiled at
his birth. The mother is real; she has suffered, waiting long;
and the father is mentioned too, for he has a share in the joy.

In the richly interwoven pattern of the vision many strains
appear — the bodings of Etruscan soothsayers; the subtleties
of Greek magic; the jollity of Sicilian shepherds; the faith of a
Hebrew prophet; the triumph of Roman conquerors; the speculations of Platonic philosophy—all contribute something to
the texture. But what is it that makes the warmth and unity
and meaning of the poem — 64 lines, all told? It is the human
affection of which a little child is the centre. This it is which
in Vergil's dream is to inspire and bless the world. "A little
child shall lead them."— lead the wild creatures of the forest
and the mountain, lead the men and women of the new era,
and save them from the wildness of the old.

> Lo, the last stage of Cumae's seer has come!
> Again the great millennial aeon dawns.
> Once more the hallowed Maid appears, once more
> Kind Saturn reigns, and from high heaven descends
> The firstborn Child of promise. Do but thou,
> Pure Goddess, by whose grace on infant eyes
> Daylight first breaks, smile softly on this babe;
> The age of iron in his time shall cease
> And golden generations fill the world.
>
> .   .   .   .
>
> For thee, fair Child, the lavish Earth shall spread
> Thy earliest playthings, trailing ivy-wreaths
> And foxgloves red and cups of water-lilies,

---

[1] *Hist. Nat.*, VII, 72; see J. F. Moulton, *Early Zoroastrianism*, 1913, p. 91, and
Early Religious Poetry of Persia, 1911, p. 51.

And wild acanthus smiling in the sun.
The goats shall come uncalled, weighed down with milk,
Nor lions' roar affright the labouring kine.
Thy very cradle, blossoming for joy,
Shall with soft buds caress thy baby face;
The treacherous snake and deadly herb shall die,
And Syrian spikenard blow on every bank.

. . . .

The field shall thrive unharrowed, vines unpruned,
And stalwart ploughmen set their oxen free.
Wool shall not learn the dyer's cozening art,
But in the meadow, on the ram's own back,
Nature shall give new colours to the fleece,
Soft blushing glow of crimson, gold of crocus,
And lambs be clothed in scarlet as they feed.
"Run, run, ye spindles! On to this fulfilment
Speed the world's fortune, draw the living thread."
So heaven's unshaken ordinance declaring
The sister Fates enthroned together sang.

Come then, dear Child of gods, Jove's mighty heir,
Begin thy high career; the hour is sounding.
See how it shakes the vaulted firmament,
Earth and the spreading seas and depth of sky!
See, in the dawning of a new creation
The heart of all things living throbs with joy!

. . . .

Come, little Child, greet with a smile thy mother!
Ten weary waiting months her love has known.
Come, little Child! Whoso is born in sorrow
Jove ne'er hath bidden join the immortal banquet,
Nor deathless Hebe deigned to be his bride.

IV

THE HOUSE OF THE HIGH PRIEST

FEW things are less interesting to most of us than the restoration of other people's ancient monuments, however proud we may be of our own; and the statement which Augustus makes in his autobiography,[1] that he 'restored 82 temples in Rome which had become ruinous by age,' is read by a modern student with a cold, or merely critical, eye. And when we find Horace warning his countrymen that they will continue to pay penalties for their fathers' sins unless and until they restore the shrines of the gods,[2] our first thought is to wonder whether Horace believed it, and our second, whether anybody else did. So far have we travelled from the feeling of the Vergilian age. Yet we must travel back again in imagination if we wish to realise what that age of men did for the world they knew, and so ultimately for us, their successors and heirs.

One of the most direct records of the sentiment of Horace's time, perhaps in some ways even more convincing than the well-known ode in Book III just referred to (which was written later), and even more striking from a practical point of view than Vergil's famous picture of this restoration as the crowning act of the triumph of Octavian *augustus* (that is, the Venerable), as Vergil then entitled him,[3] is the appeal made by Horace[4] some time between 39 and 33 B.C., in his own humorous way, to men of wealth, to spend it, not on freaks and pleasures, but on rebuilding the temples of the gods. It is the earliest

[1] The *Monumentum Ancyranum*, one of the great re-discoveries of the nineteenth century, edited by Mommsen (*Res Gestae divi Augusti*); 2d ed., Berlin, 1883.

[2] *Donec templa refeceris* is the keynote of *Odes*, III, 6.

[3] This assumes the truth of Dr. Warde Fowler's alluring conjecture, that in *Aen.*, VIII, 678, the adjective ought still to be written without any capital letter; *i. e.*, that it was either at Vergil's suggestion, or at least with his cogent support, that the name was bestowed on Octavian in 27 B.C. See Warde Fowler's *Aeneas at the Site of Rome*, 1917, p. 110.

[4] *Satires*, II, 2. 103.

13. New Fragment of Fasti (left-hand half)

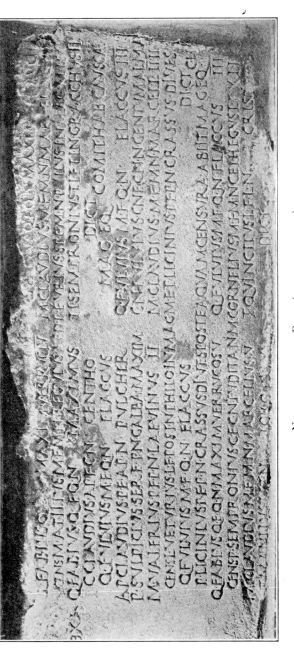

14. New fragment of Fasti (right-hand half)

case in which we find Horace working, with and for his patron
Maecenas and with his friend Vergil, to inspire his readers with
sympathy for some of the practical designs of the best minds of
his day, including the young Octavian, still poor in resources
and struggling for political pre-eminence. And the kind of effect which such appeals produced is illustrated for us by the
fortunes of a famous temple, which to a Roman of that day was
much like what the Panthéon is to a Parisian, or Westminster
Abbey to an Englishman, in our own. The story of its restoration, by private munificence but no doubt at Octavian's entreaty, is well attested; and a fragment of the new building,
hitherto unknown, and valuable for its own sake, was discovered in Rome in 1925.

The discovery adds nothing of any picturesque interest to
our knowledge; but besides completing and confirming information from different sources which we already possess, it
illustrates the nature of the evidence on which the whole system of pre-Christian chronology is based; and among the men
of whose office it brings us the official record, there are two or
three who figured in some of the most characteristic stories of
Roman history.

The block of marble just found — of which Plates 13 and 14
show the two halves [1] — comes straight down to us from 36
B.C., when the great historical monument of which it forms
a part was set up in the course of the restorative policy of
Octavian, then supreme in Rome, though he was not yet Emperor; for Mark Antony still claimed a share in the Empire,
and continued to do so until the Battle of Actium in 31 B.C.

In our schooldays we mostly regarded dates as afflictions
rather than blessings; but in any case we looked on them as
having come straight into our schoolbooks from Heaven (or
elsewhere) — things that were settled past all dispute and that
needed only to be mercifully administered in sufficiently mod-

---

[1] The numeral signs Ð XL, which appear in the margin of each of these photographs, occur only once on the stone, in the blank space in the middle. They refer,
as we shall see, to the second half. The bar across the first sign was a convenient
mark used by Roman stone-cutters to show that the sign in question was to be read
as a numeral, not a letter. From this has come the line which we (and the Italians)
draw through our L (for *libra*, 'pound') to show that it denotes a particular coin,
though the English pound has come to be a different thing from the Italian lira.

erate doses by our seniors. If we had guessed that practically every one of the figures which were given us to learn in ancient history was the result of a complex constructive process carried out by different scholars, — often involving prolonged discussion, — we might have regarded them with less respect but more interest.

The fragment of what are called the *Fasti Consulares* which has just been identified at Rome is a new part of the best basis we have for dating events of the history of the Roman Republic; and it shows very well what that basis really is. The block of marble (Plates 13 and 14) lay embedded in the ground for many centuries with other ruins of the Roman Forum; but it must have been turned out of its resting-place some two hundred years ago or earlier, and then built into the porch of a nobleman's palace at Rome (21 Via Torre Argentina). Here it was noticed a few months ago by an Italian scholar, Professor P. Mingazzini, who has just published an account of it.[1] As we shall see, it is a welcome addition to other remains of the same monument, which were discovered in the year 1546 and arranged by Michael Angelo in the form in which they stand to-day in the Capitoline Museum at Rome.

Plate 15 is taken from a sketch by Detlessen, made to show the general character of the building on which this block originally stood. It was called the Regia, or King's Palace, a name which descends from the earliest period when Rome was ruled by kings. But under the Republic the building was the official headquarters of the Pontifex Maximus, or High Priest, the head of the state religion. Among the duties discharged by him and his colleagues was the regulation of everything that concerned the Kalendar, including the official record of the names of the chief officers of state, of the census held at regular intervals, and also of the triumphs celebrated by Roman generals over the enemies of Rome. These lists were continually made up to date and preserved in the Regia. We know,

---

[1] *Notizie degli Scavi*, 1925, p. 376. A preliminary account of it was given in the *Morning Post* of London of March 16, 1926; the photograph I owe to the kindness of Professor Paribeni, the Director of the Museo delle Terme at Rome; and it was published in an article on which this chapter is based in the August number of *Discovery*, 1926.

CONSVLVM   CONSVLVM TRIVMPHORVM CONSVLVM TRIVMPHORVM TRIVMPH. CONSVLVM TRIVMPH.
   TAB. I   TAB. II   TAB. III   PAR. I   TAB. III   PAR. III   PAR. IV
                                        TAB. III   PAR. II   TAB. IV   PAR. IV

15. THE REGIA RESTORED

however, that they were re-copied (not to say re-constructed) on more than one occasion — for instance, after the burning of Rome by the Gauls in 390 B.C.; and in the course of the gen- eral restoration of ruinous or dilapidated temples in Rome in the Vergilian age the whole Regia was rebuilt, and its records set up in a more splendid form than ever before, deeply cut in letters three fifths of an inch high, on blocks of fine marble twenty inches thick, like the present specimen, which is about a foot broad, and four feet four inches long. The great thickness of the stone contributed to the solidity of the building of which it formed a part. The Regia stood in the Forum, close to the southeast end, near the Temple of Vesta; and the list of consuls was contained in the four tables or panels shown in Detlessen's sketch. The list of Triumphs was cut on the face of four columns on one side. Of the four panels, the two which are on the side of the building took the form of what we should call blind windows; the best-preserved of all is the third, that is, the first of those on the side wall, which Plate 16 represents in the shape to which it had been restored by the labours of many scholars before the present discovery. (The figures in the margin, of course, are not part of the monument; but I have added them to show the reader the dates of the years covered by the record.)

Now observe the gap between Fragment XVI, *a* and *b*, and Fragment XVII, *a* and *b*. As the monument stood till the new discovery, it gave us no record of the consuls in two periods of time: those from 278 to 266 B.C. were on the slab missing from the first column; those from 214 to 208 B.C. were on that missing from the second column. The block newly found supplies this gap almost completely,[1] and will shortly be put into its place with the rest; and then visitors to Rome will be able to see the whole panel in just the shape (save for some slight breaks) which was seen every day by Vergil and Horace and Livy and all the other citizens of Rome, to whom the beauty and stateliness of the new building betokened the restoration of order and peace, after a century of civil wars.

[1] One line is lost on the left and two on the right, at the top; at the bottom, two lines are lost on the left and one and a half on the right.

"But how do we know," the reader will ask, "that the dates you have put in the margin are the dates in which these different people respectively held office?" The answer is contained in 340 folio pages of the second edition of Volume I of the *Corpus Inscriptionum Latinarum*, in which two or three pupils of Mommsen, of whom Wilhelm Henzen was the chief, collected and arranged in a splendid series of tables, based on Mommsen's own work in the first edition of the same *Corpus*, all the evidence[1] from different sources bearing on each one of the dates, carefully discussing doubtful points. The list of consuls in its briefest form occupies sixty-nine folio pages. Side by side with the record in this inscription, or batch of inscriptions, which, as we shall see, represents the official tradition of 36 B.C., Mommsen and his pupils have set the accounts preserved in six or seven other sources; the chief of these is Livy's great history, with late writers like Cassiodorus, who drew from Livy and whose summaries are especially valuable for the long periods covered by the parts of Livy's history which have disappeared.

On so huge and thorny a subject I hardly dare to enter here. But a single example, taken from the newly discovered fragment, will show the enormous help which these official *Fasti* have given us in the task of determining the actual dates. The second line of the right-hand column of Plate 13 gives us as the name of one of the Consuls in a particular year (277 B.C.): C. IVNIVS. C. F. C. N. BVBVLCVS. BRVTVS. II; that is to say, 'Gaius Junius Bubulcus Brutus, son of Gaius and grandson of [an older] Gaius, Consul for the second time.' Now, his consulship falls in a period for which Livy's record is lost. It was contained in some one of the books between XI and XX — books which, as you will remember, three years ago that curious person, Dr. Di Martino, professed to have found and to be copying out! According to Cassiodorus, the Consul's name was Gaius Junius; two other summaries give his name merely as Bubulcus; a third summariser gives it as Brutus. This official record for the first time shows us what the man's full name

[1] That is to say, all the evidence available before 1893, when this edition was published.

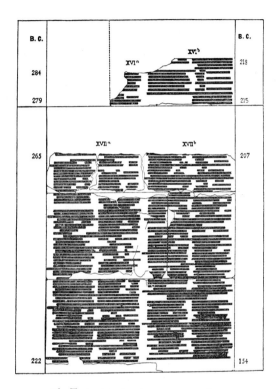

16. THE POSITION OF THE FRAGMENTS

really was, and shows also that the other records were perfectly correct, — so far as they went, — though each of them was incomplete. It would take long to explain fully the apparent discrepancy; here it will be enough to say that one of the commonest methods of forming a list was to mention only the cognomen, that is, the third name, of each person. This was no doubt the form in which schoolboys had to learn them by heart; and phrases like Horace's *consule Planco* (his full name was Lucius Munatius Plancus) probably represent the way in which most Romans thought of any date in Roman history. I should add, however, that the figure ÐXL, opposite the Consuls for what we call 214 B.C., gives us the official Roman view of the number of that year as counted from the foundation of Rome. This view we know was based on the computations of Varro, the famous scholar of Cicero's day.

One is tempted to linger on a multitude of other topics, full of interest to any student of Roman life, and suggested by this newly found trace of Octavian's pleasant taste for putting things in order; but I can touch upon only one or two.

How do we know that this list of consuls was set up in 36 B.C.? The answer is curious, and gives us an intimate view of the mind of that young ruler at different periods of his career. The whole list, as we have it, goes down to the year A.D. 12, and therefore, of course, includes the Consuls for the year 37 B.C., of whom Mark Antony was one (during a period of temporary reconciliation with Octavian). The list also contains the name of his grandfather, — an earlier Marcus Antonius, the orator, — who is entered as having been Censor in 97 B.C. But there is a curious feature in these entries — the names have been erased, and then re-cut deeper in the stone. The name of the grandfather has been re-cut at a slightly different part of the line, so that the traces of the beginning of the name left by the incision appear on the left, and then the full name cut deeper into the marble farther to the right. What does this mean? It means what we are told by more than one historian, that after the Battle of Actium orders were given for the names of Antony and his ancestors to be everywhere removed from the *Fasti*. It means also, as we learn further from our authorities,[1] that the names were restored by Augustus at a later period of his reign, when he had learnt much from experience, and more still from his friends and inspirers, the poets Vergil and Horace. Thus he escaped, or at least cancelled, an evil memory such as, two centuries later, the brutal Caracallus attached for ever to his own name by causing to be erased from public monuments all over the Empire[2] the name of his younger brother, Geta, whom he had murdered. Further, since in 31 B.C. the names needed to be removed to meet Octavian's desire at the time, they must have been cut originally before 31 B.C., and yet at some time after Antony had been Consul in 37 B.C.; and since we know that the Regia was rebuilt by Domitius Calvinus in 36 B.C. (out of money which he brought home from his Spanish province), there is no reason to doubt that the list down to that date was then set up and continued from year to year later on.[3]

An amusing story is preserved by Dio[4] which shows both Octavian's interest in the restoration and his difficulty in finding money at that time. Domitius desired that the interior of the restored temple should be handsomely furnished with statues, at all events for the ceremony of its dedication, and begged Octavian to help. Octavian, not being able to purchase what was needed, promised to lend him some of those which he possessed, acquired probably by inheritance from the Dictator Julius, and accordingly had the statues conveyed down to the Forum and set up in the new building. Some time after, he asked Domitius to send them back, as he missed them in his own house (or gardens?). Domitius replied that he was no longer in office and had no public workmen at his disposal; but that, if Octavian would arrange with a contractor to fetch them, they should be at his disposal. Octavian left them

---

[1] Especially Tacitus, *Annals*, III, 18.

[2] For example, on the Arch of Severus still standing in the Forum, and on the monument to Severus, Caracallus, and Geta, which it fell to me to identify when it came to light at Ribchester in 1908 (*Class. Rev.*, XXII [1908], 196).

[3] This summary statement represents the central facts; but it excludes all reference to details, such as the date of the Table of Triumphs.

[4] Dio, XLVIII, 42. 5.

where they were, partly, perhaps, as Dio tells us, because he feared to be guilty of sacrilege.

Let me add a few sentences to enable the reader to identify the genial personality mentioned in the last line but one of Plate 14 — Marcus Claudius Marcellus, who is there recorded as Consul for the fifth time; the year was 208 B.c. Rather curiously, the Table does not mention the fact of his tragic death before the end of the year — though this is usually stated in such cases, with the name of the man chosen to fill the vacancy. Yet some later hand has added in smaller letters to the name of his colleague, Titus Quinctus Crispinus, the abbreviated phrase EX VOL — followed, no doubt, before the stone was damaged, by M. E.; that is to say, *ex volnere* [or *volneribus*] *mortuus est* ('he died of a wound, or wounds'.) These wounds, Livy tells[1] us, were received in the engagement in which Marcellus himself was slain; both Consuls took part in a reconnaissance, and were overwhelmed by a large force which Hannibal had put in ambush. Perhaps the reason for the silence of the *Fasti* was that this had happened so late in the year (208 B.c.) that no one was appointed to fill his place for the remaining days. But the name alone is enough to bring to every student of Roman history the recollection of a proud and sturdy warrior, who alone of Roman generals in those ten years had more than once fought a serious battle with Hannibal without suffering disaster; and who, more even than Fabius the Delayer, had helped to restore the confidence which the Romans had lost after the terrible defeats of Trebia, Trasimene, and Cannae. Marcellus, too, it was who finally drove out the Carthaginians from Sicily and established Roman authority in that island; and who, though he carried off a multitude of Greek statues as trophies from the island, was nevertheless so revered and trusted by the Sicilians that, when they sent a deputation to the Senate to ask for more indulgent terms of peace than he had granted them, the deputation ended by begging Marcellus and his family after him for ever to be the official patrons and protectors of Sicily at Rome.

One incident in his capture of Syracuse, though it is per-

[1] Livy, XXVII, 27.

haps too familiar to need re-telling, is of interest as showing the respect which the Romans felt for Greek learning even when they had suffered from it. The great astronomer and mathematician Archimedes was living in Syracuse when Marcellus assailed it in 214 B.C.;[1] and he devised powerful machines, both for hurling bullets to a surprising distance from the walls, and for lowering chains with great tongs attached, which gripped and pulled out of the water the prows of ships attacking the town from the harbour, and then suddenly let them fall again. By such means he baffled all the efforts of the Romans to storm the town. When it finally surrendered, after two years' siege, a Roman soldier, hunting for booty, found Archimedes poring over a geometrical design which he had traced in sand on the floor of his room. Thinking that the astronomer was extracting some treasure from its hiding-place, the soldier killed him. Marcellus heard of his death with indignation, and not only buried the great discoverer with a splendid funeral, but took steps to secure that his family should be placed out of reach of want and treated with honour.

This story Livy related with keen interest and sympathy, and also, we may be sure, with especial pleasure, for two reasons. It did honour to the great house of the Marcelli, so closely allied to Augustus, and helped, in Livy's delicate way,[2] to console him in the great bereavement which he had suffered in the death of the young Marcellus, his nephew and chosen heir. But a duty even more congenial to the great student and historian was to describe the homage paid to learning by a conqueror, a relation between power and thought which it was the especial distinction of Livy's own generation to have known again in Rome.

[1] Livy, XXIV, 34.
[2] This assumes that Book XXIV was written after 23 B.C. If it was written earlier, while Marcellus still lived, the honour to his ancestry would be not less appropriate. On the death of the young Marcellus, see p. 147.

V

AN UNNOTICED ASPECT OF VERGIL'S PERSONALITY [1]

LIKE other great writers, Vergil has suffered something from his popularity; the fact that he has been read in schools for centuries has made the meaning of his writings as a whole fairly clear, but has also, perhaps inevitably, tended to throw into the shade not a few finer points of interpretation, on which a great deal of the deepest understanding of his poetry must, after all, depend. That there are plenty of difficult passages every schoolboy, and still more every teacher, knows well; but in all there has grown up what one might call an "authorised version," from which the individual teacher, however many doubts he may feel, hesitates to depart. Most of us, I think, are familiar with the effect which this situation has upon a class of schoolboys, who are exceedingly quick to see whether their teacher really believes what he is putting before them; and a good deal, though not all,[2] of the distaste which schoolboys are sometimes said to feel for Vergil — a distaste which, if it really exists, must surely be regarded as a disgrace to their teachers — is due, I believe, to this acquiescence in formulae which do not in reality represent all that can be known, in the light of modern scholarship, about the central figure of Roman literature.

[1] Much of this paper was included in a lecture delivered in October, 1906, before the Classical Association, in Manchester, England, and first published in the Proceedings of that meeting. The proposed interpretation of *Georgics*, I, 24–42, was cited, and the exordium of the *Culex* briefly compared with it in *Great Inheritance*, London, 1921, p. 82. In its present form, the paper represents teaching given to my Vergil class at Harvard in the spring of 1927.

[2] Some trouble, no doubt, will always be caused, especially to younger or duller pupils, by the subtlety and richness of a style in which it is rare to find a statement, or even a phrase, which does not carry by suggestion a good deal more meaning than it does on the surface. One result of this is that no translation into prose, in any language, can ever represent more than a part, and sometimes not more than a fractional part, of what was in Vergil's mind.

It may be, however, that some will doubt the truth of this contention; and everyone will be rightly sceptical of the attempt to discover new meanings in passages which might be thought as plain as they are familiar. Let me remind any such persons that as recently as 1901 a new name was added to the list of surviving Latin poets by the late Professor Franz Skutsch of Breslau, who demonstrated [1] that the poem called the *Ciris*, by tradition ascribed to Vergil, is (mainly at least) the work of Cornelius Gallus. Or take a smaller point. For how many centuries, I wonder, have schoolboys and others been forced to translate *habent acies* by "lead men into battle," because Professor D. A. Slater and Dr. Warde Fowler [2] had not yet shown its meaning in the passage

> hi Fescenninas *acies* Aequosque Faliscos,
> hi Soractis *habent* arces [3]

to be the same as that of the English word with which it is identical, the Derbyshire "edge" — that is, a ridge ending a high plateau? Or, to give as an instance a question which has only recently been asked: why is it that Vergil opened the Sixth Book of the *Aeneid* — that profound poem in which, like Shakespeare in his *Tempest*, he centred his whole history and vision of human life — with stories of primitive Crete (*in foribus letum Androgeo*)? Surely because Vergil knew by tradition what we have been willing to learn only from the sharp spades of Sir Arthur Evans, that Crete was the earliest home of European civilisation.

"Vergil," said Dr. T. E. Page, in a brilliant speech, at the first meeting of the Classical Association in 1904 — "Vergil in his shy way would remind us that he is first of all a poet." It is a few cases of this characteristic shyness, concealing more thought than has been yet understood, which we are now to consider. And I must ask one indulgence at the outset. It is impossible to put into words the suggestions implicit in these passages without giving them just the dogmatic, prosaic colour

[1] In his two books, *Aus Vergils Frühzeit*, Leipzig, 1901, and *Vergil und Gallus*, Leipzig, 1905.
[2] See *Class. Rev.*, XIX (1905), 38, and XXXI (1917), 20, and Warde Fowler's *Vergil's Gathering of the Clans*, Oxford, 1916, p. 64.
[3] *Aen.*, VII, 695.

which Vergil avoided; but I hope it will be believed that I am conscious of this, and that Dr. Page's dictum is one which I have taken to heart.

Let us begin with one or two examples of this reticence or gentleness of tone in utterances on grave matters. A typical case is the tribute to the philosophic research of Lucretius in the Second Book of the *Georgics* (*felix qui potuit*, and so forth), followed immediately by the resolute declaration of the theoretically inferior but really more delightful calling of the plain lover of the country.[1] Or I might point to the closing scene of the *Aeneid*, in which the hesitation of Aeneas, whether or not to spare the conquered Turnus, reflects the poet's own doubt as to the efficacy of force as a remedy. Vergil characteristically departs from the Homeric formula, which pictures the spirit of a slain warrior as 'groaning over its own fate at leaving manhood and youth behind' (ὃν πότμον γοόωσα, λιποῦσ' ἀδροτῆτα καὶ ἥβην). In Vergil the groan is there, —

uitaque cum gemitu fugit indignata sub umbras, —

but the merely selfish side of it, which to Homer was the chief point of the pathos (ὃν πότμον), is in Vergil suppressed, and instead we have the striking word *indignata*, not 'groaning' merely, but 'indignant.' Why does Vergil stop to regard this 'indignation' of the dying rebel? Surely it suggests the other side of every forceful triumph. This will not be strange to those who have realised the whole spirit of the story in the second half of the *Aeneid*, with its standing contrast between the merciful, humane Aeneas and the weak and overbearing personalities, whether of gods or men, who break with violence the course of his duty.

There are quite a number of passages which have one thing in common, namely, that Vergil seems to halt between two or more opinions. In all of them I cannot help thinking that his real opinion is discernible, notwithstanding the hesitation, and that Vergil's hope in expressing his hesitation was to enlist the reader's sympathy on that side better than could be done

---

[1] Vergil's relation to Lucretius is discussed in *Great Inheritance*, pp. 102 f., and in Chapter 7, below; and his attitude to Nature, in chap. 2 of the earlier book (cf. p. 109, below).

by any direct, dogmatic declaration. One of these is in the
Fifth Book of the *Aeneid*. When Aeneas is offering sacrifice at
the tomb of his father Anchises, he is cheered by a special portent: a snake appears from under the altar, which is also the
tomb, and, encircling the altar, devours the offerings upon it,
and then retires whence it had come, doing no harm to anyone. Now why is this incident brought in? Clearly, says the
reader who knows anything of Greek customs, because the
connexion of snakes with tombs was an ancient Greek tradition, continually represented in Greek sculpture; and the em-
blem is commonly interpreted by modern scholars as at all
events connected with some belief in an after-life. We need
hardly stop to remember the physical origin of this belief; the
dryness of the shelter which the tombs afforded was probably
as congenial to a snake at Athens as on the Quantocks today,
to say nothing of the offerings of food. But this is not the
point. The point is, what did Aeneas think? Aeneas hesitates
(l. 95) —

> incertus, geniumne loci famulumne parentis
> esse putet.

He does not know 'whether the snake is the genius of the
place,' — that is to say, is itself the embodiment of his father's
spirit (this being no doubt a popular belief), — or whether
it is only 'some attendant creature that waits upon his father'
in the Underworld. Surely, when the question is once asked,
it is quite clear what Vergil meant, and what he did not say.
He meant to suggest a less gross and more poetic interpretation
of the snake at the tomb; but he is so gently considerate of the
ancient superstition that he will not put his criticism of it in
any more positive form. This passage in itself is of no great
importance; but it is typical of Vergil's method of suggest-
ing, rather than explicitly teaching, what he wished his readers
to believe.[1]

The next example is one of larger scope, and is suggested by
a criticism of Charles James Fox. After reading the Fourth
Book of the *Aeneid*, he exclaimed to a friend, "Can you bear

---

[1] Other examples of hesitation (which I believe to be of the same kind) in the
Aeneid are discussed below, in Chapter 7, p. 100. (*Aen.*, IX, 184; II, 738, 739;
III, 262; X, 109–110).

this?" adding that Aeneas was "always either insipid or odious." One may search in vain for any justification of these epithets through the speeches of Aeneas in that Book and all his action after he receives the command to go. Every word and movement is full of pity and consideration for Dido, of sorrow for himself, limited only by obedience to his divine commission. What is it, then, that produced the feeling to which Fox has given such blunt expression? Clearly, the whole situation; the demands made by an imperial emergency, not merely for the sacrifice of personal happiness, but for the wreck of a great woman's life. Fox is not alone in being moved by indignant pity; but he surely ought to be alone in regarding as a reproach to a great artist the very first feeling which that artist's work awakens. Is it wise to assume that the artist's own intention had no share in the result? Let Dido's appeal [1] to Aeneas, or even its last four lines, teach us more truly what Vergil felt:

> saltem si qua mihi de te suscepta fuisset
> ante fugam suboles, si quis mihi paruolus aula
> luderet Aeneas, qui te tamen ore referret,
> non equidem omnino capta ac deserta uiderer.

> Ah, but if first, ere thou had'st fled, one ray
> Of gentler hope had dawned, if in this court
> A baby child of ours had danced and smiled,
> Smiling his far-off father back again,
> Ah then, methinks, I were not, as I am,
> Utterly, utterly betrayed, undone.

These are lines whose meaning no one knows fully till he has passed through some one of the darker shadows of human existence. Who can believe that the poet who conceived this appeal had nothing but approval for the conventional view of such a drama? That view is represented in part of the reply of Aeneas; but Vergil's own comment is in what Aeneas does not say, in what he tacitly admits, and in the sequel. The slow, mournful syllables of the half-line which is Aeneas' last word —

> Italiam non sponte sequor —

---

[1] The whole speech is rendered in *Great Inheritance*, chap. 7, where the evidence for the interpretation here suggested will be found.

echo the sorrow of men and women doomed by political pressure to destroy their dearest ties. The truth, whose weight has been felt, but not understood, is that Vergil's whole story of Dido is a poetic but profound demonstration of the cruelty of certain ideas current then, and largely current now, which lie at the root of the tragedy.

The last point which I will ask you now to consider is one in which Vergil's feeling has exercised no small influence on human thought; but through the delicate, evasive colour of his teaching it has never been realised that the influence was Vergil's at all. It is one of the most important — perhaps the most important — of all Vergil's contributions to the ethics of Christendom. And yet the passage to which I must especially refer is the one in all his writings which is read with most surprise, not to say amazement, by modern students. Put in the form of a question, what we are to ask is this: what did Vergil mean by deifying Augustus? In what sense did Vergil comply with the literary fashion of his day? [1]

That that was the fashion needs no demonstration; but let us compare the manner of it in Vergil and in other poets under the Empire. We need not stop to quote the unpleasant use to which, a century later, the custom was applied by such a parasite as Martial — *non ragionam di lor*. But when we find Propertius using the word *deus* as a synonym for Augustus (*lacrimas uidimus ire deo*), we feel at once that there is no parallel to this in Vergil, even in his earliest Eclogue. In Horace, whose prophecy that Augustus will one day drink nectar at the celestial table is at least not lacking in dignity, we hear a strain less ethereal than Vergil's, though in purpose not different. The first appearance of Octavian as divine in Vergil[2] is when he has promised peace in place of ruin to the Mantuan farmer (*deus nobis haec otia fecit*). At the end of the First Book of the *Georgics*[3] the courts of Heaven are said to envy earth her possession of such a hero — but why? Because he is to save Rome and the world from utter overthrow (*euerso saeclo*) — as

---

[1] The object of what follows is not to discuss the general aspects, or the ultimate fruits of this fashion, but to make clear the limits within which it was sanctioned by Vergil.

[2] *Ecl.*, I, 6; see p. 32 and Chapter 2 generally.   [3] I, 500-503.

of course he did. And so through all the *Aeneid*, wherever
Augustus is made divine, it is because he is saving mankind
from the horrors of the anarchic century that was ended by the
battle of Actium. The two ideas are inseparably linked; when-
ever Augustus puts on the robes of a god, it is to do hard work
for men.[1]

Yet there is one well-known passage that seems an exception
to this rule, a passage in which the deification takes a poetic
form repellent to the modern reader. In the exordium of the
Georgics[2] Augustus is invited, not merely to become a god, but
to choose for himself some particular type of deity — a ludi-
crous combination, according to our modern commentators, of
polytheism, anthropomorphism, and the grossest court flat-
tery. As usual, those who condemn most loudly have understood least; some of them, who have mocked at Vergil's
astronomy, might have waited to read the ancient commentaries, in which they would have found enlightenment; and all
of them might have asked what Vergil did elsewhere under
similar conditions. One would have expected any would-be
interpreter of this prologue at least to compare it with two
other prologues which Vergil has left us, and which exhibit
some parallel features of structure likely to give us help.

In the *Culex* the first eleven lines give us the name of the
young patron (Octavius) to whom the poem is addressed, and
its subject, with a promise of greater efforts later on; the next
twelve invoke suitable aid from Phoebus, the Naiads of
Pieria, and the rustic deity, Pales; the next twelve enumerate
certain topics — the war of the Giants; the war of the Centaurs with the Lapithae; and the First and Second Persian
Wars — which the poet will not choose; and the last five pray
for blessings on his patron — forty lines in all.

In Book III of the *Georgics* the first two lines declare the subject, namely, flocks and herds, under the names of two deities,
Pales and the 'shepherd from Amphrysus' and the 'wood-
lands and rivers'of Arcadia. The next five reject briefly a number of subjects, familiar in tragedy and the Alexandrine school

---

[1] The late Dr. Warde Fowler accepted this view in *Roman Ideas of Deity*, London, 1914, p. 104.   [2] I, 24-42.

8-90

of epic (or epyllian) poetry. Then a striking passage of thirty-two lines describes what Vergil will one day do, in building a marble temple of poetry which shall make Mantua famous through the tribute of a Mantuan poet to the triumphs of Caesar over Britain, India, Armenia, and Parthia, to his Trojan lineage, and to his punishment of treason. The fortieth line brings us back, with five others, to the immediate subject in which Maecenas will help him, the beasts of pasture, dogs, and horses; yet three more are added, promising ere long to sing of the glories of Caesar, his patron to be — forty-eight lines in all.

Pietas

The proportion of space thus allotted to the various topics differs, naturally, from that in the *Culex*. But the character and order of the thought is the same — first the subject of the book, and the deities connected with it; then the topics rejected or deferred; then the patron and his relation to the chosen theme.

Now what have we in Book I? First the subject, in four lines, and the name of his patron, Maecenas; then the deities proper to the theme, in nineteen lines; then nineteen more, invoking a greater patron, Caesar — forty-two lines in all.

It will hardly be denied that in their general design the three proems have a parallel character which is striking; but that of the First Book seems to differ in one respect. So far as we have yet examined it, we have found no enumeration of topics rejected or deferred. Is it there?

Of what does the invocation to Caesar consist? It presents to him a choice of five alternatives; and to Vergil's readers a riddle not yet solved. What is Vergil's question? He asks, apparently, over which realm of nature Caesar is to reign: the earth (which includes both land and men), the ocean, the stars, or, finally, the world of the dead. The last suggestion the poet seems to withdraw as soon as it is made, and yet to withdraw with reluctance, in one of the most complex sentences that ever baffled a schoolboy and his teachers (ll. 36–42):

quidquid eris, — nam te nec sperant Tartara regem
nec tibi regnandi ueniat tam dira cupido,
(quamuis Elysios miretur Graecia campos
nec repetita sequi curet Proserpina matrem) —

da facilem cursum atque audacibus adnue coeptis
ignarosque uiae mecum miseratus agrestis
ingredere et uotis iam nunc adsuesce uocari.

What does this mean? Can we not all remember the perplexity
with which we first gazed upon this parenthesis within a
parenthesis? For what conceivable reason does Vergil dwell
on the attractions of an alternative which he has admitted to
be inappropriate, and which to us seems merely absurd? And
what have Greece and Proserpine to do with a Roman emperor?

The key to all this lies, I believe, in the concluding lines.
Augustus is to decide upon the sphere first proposed to him;
he is to be a god of earth. To what end? To help Vergil in his
great task of reviving country life in Italy; in other words, the
influence and encouragement on which the poet relies are to be
devoted to a poem on agriculture. The hesitation that Vergil
felt is as to the subject of the poem for which he is to seek
the Emperor's approval. Shall he write of agriculture, like
Varro? Of the growth of civilisation, like Lucretius? Of
geography and ocean exploration, like Strabo? Of astronomy,
like Aratus, Manilius, Hyginus? Or of the mysteries of creation and the after-life? He had done so before in the *Culex*
and the *Song of Silenus*, and in an early poem on Orpheus,
destined to be embodied,[1] for sad reasons, in the Fourth Book
of the *Georgics;* so did the bard who sang to Dido at Carthage;
so Vergil dreamed already of doing, to crown his life's work,
in some majestic vision like the Sixth Book of the *Aeneid*, in
which all the lore of Greek philosophy and all the wealth of
Greek fancy were to be blended with the deep patriotism and
the deeper humanity of the greatest poet of Italy.

This interpretation of the close of the passage "admits of no
doubt, and it carries the rest."[2] This passage, therefore, is
not an exception, but an example of the principle for which I
am pleading. Augustus becomes a god that he may do some
vital service to the world of men.

[1] See "The Fall of Cornelius Gallus," in *Great Inheritance*, chap. 5.
[2] This comment on the theory was made by the late Professor S. H. Butcher, at
Manchester, at the close of the lecture.

"Poor pagan Vergil!" sigh our Christian commentators; "He could not help yielding to the superstition of his day." Have those who thus teach studied sufficiently the meaning of the word *deus?* Have they considered the catalogue of personalities and of things too contemptible and trivial to be called personalities at all, among which the use of the word enrolled Octavian? Between the Latin *deus* and the English *God* stretches a gulf of nineteen centuries of Christian teaching. Auguste Comte himself could find no better weapon against all that he counted superstition than the worship of great men who had served mankind. By accepting the deification of Augustus in his action as a supreme human benefactor, Vergil did a service to humanity; for the implicit picture of what a god ought to be was one step by which mankind was lifted toward that divine ideal of manhood which began to be unfolded only nineteen years after Vergil's heart had ceased to beat.

VI

UNDER HANNIBAL'S SHADOW [1]

FEW of us are too young, and certainly no one of us is too old, to be able to look back on the four years of the European war as an experience standing by itself, sharply marked off from the rest of our lives. And one of the ways in which it differs, probably, from any other four years through which we have passed is that we have comparatively clear conceptions of what then happened to us as a nation.

Even now it may be that the chronological order of some things is fading from memory; but the great events and sufferings of the period are still present in our minds and still among the things which help to shape our political judgement. Probably never before those four years had we possessed in our own experience anything that we could call knowledge of what our nation was; and what conceptions we had attached to the names of foreign nations were even more vague or fragmentary. But under the shocks and stress of the war every one of us became conscious of the larger organism of which he was a part. As a nation we found ourselves, and we have not yet ceased to be self-conscious. Most of us, indeed, have fallen into the habit of connecting in our own minds many of the details of our daily experience with this new consciousness which has been forced upon us. It has chanced that since then one of my own duties has been to study Livy's record of the long struggle between Rome and Carthage some twenty-one centuries ago. That contest, which lasted sixteen years, shows certain features not without parallels in our own shorter ordeal. Both likenesses and differences may be worth our notice, especially

[1] This lecture was first delivered at the John Rylands Library at Manchester, on October 10, 1923. To my friend Mr. Donald Atkinson, M.A., Reader in Ancient History in the University of Manchester, I am greatly indebted for kind criticism which has removed more than one inaccuracy.

if they can help us at all toward building up that more true
and just and enduring conception of national life, — indeed, of
civilised life as a whole, — which is what we all earnestly, even
though unconsciously, desire to reach, when we ponder on the
war and its issues. Most of us are rather shy of moralising;
and since the temptation is supposed to be especially ensnar-
ing to professors, let me try to escape it by the old Cambridge
habit of sticking closely to my text (I mean to the stories which
Livy tells us), and by leaving them to suggest their own moral.

The period represented by the title of this lecture is one of
twelve years,[1] during which Hannibal with his army was in
Italy, a standing danger to the power, and sometimes even to
the existence, of Rome. The three preceding years had been
marked by the great disasters of the Trebia, Lake Trasimene,
and Cannae, which are familiar to all students of history.
Hannibal had three times wiped out great Roman armies, and
after the last defeat, that of Cannae, in 216 B.C., men said
despairingly in Rome that there was no Roman camp left in
Italy, no Roman army, and no Roman general. Certainly for
several weeks there was no Roman army there except the gar-
rison of Rome itself. Twelve years later we find Hannibal still
unconquered, but recalled by his own government to defend
Carthage against Scipio, who had crossed to Africa, had won
various victories over the Carthaginian generals, and was to
crown these victories in the following year (202) by the defeat of Hannibal himself at the battle of Zama.

My purpose is not to trace the whole chequered story of the
Roman recovery, but rather to direct attention to a few smaller
incidents rarely mentioned by modern historians, some of
which may give us more intimate knowledge of the conduct
and feeling of the Roman people itself during these years.
And they will give us something more; for in the tone and comments of the historian, writing in the early period of the reign
of Augustus, we shall hear an echo of the feeling of that generation as they looked back upon the ordeal through which
their forefathers had passed. How familiar and how grave the
retrospect still was, we may judge from many well-known pas-

[1] 215–203 B.C.

sages [1] of Horace and of Vergil, and from Livy's striking preface to the ten Books in which he tells the story of the sixteen years of the war. It is not too much to say that that recollection was to every Roman the greatest part of the records of his country; and, like the Spanish Wars of Elizabeth in the history of England, or the War of Independence in that of New England, it made the epoch in which the Roman people finally grew into the people that later generations knew — or thought they knew — by that proud name. For the Roman people itself the disasters, the sufferings, and the victories of that war became a kind of standard or background against which they measured both the dangers and the triumphs of their own day. The whole story was an element in the national consciousness; and to understand the thought of the Vergilian Age, it is well to realise what that element was like.

Of course, in some sense, all wars are alike; both sides have always things to suffer, both sides prove themselves capable of some barbarous and some noble deeds. Difficulties of supply and transport, and failures through the incompetence of commanders, are certain to be heard of in any long war, and upon such matters we need not dwell. We may, however, note in passing, among these more external resemblances, that at the outset and long after, both we and the Romans had to contend with generalship vastly superior to anything we could find for ourselves; that both we and the Romans had difficulty in securing an adequate supply of munitions; that the armies of both were multiplied many times; and that both took extraordinary measures for meeting the financial strain. But some of our more intimate troubles, too, are not without their ancient analogues. We shall note in these twelve years the interference of political rivalries at home with the conduct of war in the field, — such as partisan attacks on particular generals; troubles with objectors to military service; troubles with allies of doubtful loyalty, — and there were remarkable reactions from the strain, not merely in the political, but also in the religious, life of the community.

[1] Horace, *Epodes*, XVI, 6; *Odes*, II, 1, III, 5, IV, 4; and Vergil, *Aen.*, IV, 625–629, VI, 846 and 859, to mention only the chief references.

Note first, for convenience, three dates which divide the period into four parts. Immediately after Cannae, in 216 B.C., the powerful city of Capua, wealthier even than Rome, threw in its lot with Hannibal. The first part of our period runs from 216 to 211 B.C., the year in which Hannibal made a dash upon Rome — though when he got there he did not venture to attack it, so strongly was the city fortified; in which the two elder Scipios were defeated and killed in Spain, so that what remained there of two Roman armies was without a commander; and in which, on the other hand, Capua, after a long siege which Hannibal found himself unable to break, surrendered to the Romans and was absolutely destroyed. These are the great events of 211. The next date is 207 B.C., when Hasdrubal, bringing a great army from Spain to reinforce his brother Hannibal, was defeated and slain at the river Metaurus. Finally, when the younger Scipio had crossed to Africa in 204, Hannibal was constrained to follow him in the next year. These dates will provide enough framework to carry a few pictures chosen from Livy's story.

In choosing them I have been mainly guided by the wish to ascertain as nearly as may be what the Romans were actually thinking and feeling; and especially to trace the instinct which seemed to guide them even in the worst moments of doubt. Some aspects of this inner life appear in incidents which Livy felt to be characteristic of the time. Little as Livy cared for precision of detail or statistics for their own sake, it is universally acknowledged that he had a singular insight into the characters of individual men and a singular power of portraying what he saw. Not less we shall realise, I hope, from the passages now to be examined, that there stood in his imagination, more clearly cut even than the portrait of any one man, the figure of the Roman nation, with its weaknesses and follies, its nobleness and strength, grown into a living whole. And even if I fail to embody in words the sense that Livy has impressed on me of this almost personal being, we shall in any case have seen something of human motive and human courage in one of the most striking epochs of the story of Europe.

We start from a position which seemed one of despair. In

the battle of Cannae, the third of three great defeats, the Romans had lost over 48,000 slain and some 5000 prisoners, the total approaching five sixths of the forces with which they began the war. Two consular armies had disappeared. The profound anxiety of the Romans appears vividly in their religious proceedings. In his history of the *Religious Experience of the Roman People*,[1] Dr. Warde Fowler has pointed out its effect in popular psychology. The gods whom the state had worshipped with punctual care, and who had brought Rome, so its citizens felt, through centuries of danger to the headship of all Italy and to the mastery of the seas around it — these gods seemed now to have changed their divine minds. How else could they suffer their worshippers to fall into so great calamity?

Throughout the period two feelings prevailed, apparently in sharp contradiction, but springing from the same root. First, a feverish desire to secure the favor of their old gods by any and every method that could be suggested, a fear which led men to look hungrily for every indication of the will of Heaven in the customary channels of omens, prophecy, and divination; and, side by side with this desire, a continual doubt of the efficacy of the old ways, and a search for newer and more powerful protectors, from whatever source the knowledge of them might be drawn. The professional exponents of established religion were quite hard-worked; always called upon to produce some religious explanation of the appalling things that were happening, and to devise some new ceremonial which might impress men's imagination with a sense of duty performed and so renew their confidence in Heaven. Livy makes clear what he himself thought of this whole business of prodigies and portents; but he makes not less clear — and this is where his insight is deeper than that of some modern writers — how indispensable to the popular mind of that century this religion was.

After the battle of Trasimene, in 217, the College of Pontiffs produced long lists of ritual duties which had been insufficiently performed; and from one of their sacred documents,

[1] Chap. 14.

which was not merely open to convenient interpolation, but offered great latitude when it came to be interpreted, — the Sibylline Books, — they ordered what was called a 'Sacred Spring,' that is, a vow payable five years hence by the whole community, which promised to offer to Jupiter every head of sheep and swine, goats and kine, that was born in that fifth spring, if the Roman state survived so long. After Cannae in 216 their despair took a more sombre form,[1] especially when it appeared that the Vestal Virgins of the year had polluted their office.

Besides these great adversities, men were put in fear with sundry prodigious tokens: and among others, in that one year, two vestal virgins, Opimia and Floronia, were detected of manifest unchastity: the one of them was buried alive, as the manner was, under the ground at the Colline Gate; the other killed herself.

The man who had committed the fault with Floronia, was by the chief Priest so beaten with rods in the Comitium, that he died under his hand. This heinous offence falling out among so many calamities, was reckoned, as usually it is, for a portentous sign; and therefore the Decemvirs were commanded to search the Sibylline Books. And Fabius Pictor was sent to Delphi, to consult with the Oracle of Apollo, and to learn by what prayers and offerings they might pacify the gods, and what would be the end of so great and fearful miseries. In the meanwhile, out of the learning contained in those Books of Destiny, there were performed certain extraordinary sacrifices: among which a Gaul together with a Gallic woman, likewise a Grecian man and woman, were let down alive in the Beast-market and shut into a vault under the ground, stoned all about: a place aforetime embrued and polluted with the blood of mankind sacrificed, a rite most unnatural to the religion of the Romans. When they had sufficiently (as they thought) pacified the gods,

they turned to matters of war, so Livy concludes. Note his phrase, 'as they thought,' and his disgust at the barbarous use of human sacrifice. *Tantum religio potuit suadere malorum*, when the whole community was acting under stress of fear.

Every year we find a set of prodigies recorded and expiated at great cost; as Livy tells us,[2] the demand created the supply:

---

[1] Livy, XXII, 57. 6. My renderings of Livy are based on the Elizabethan version of Philemon Holland.
[2] XXIV, 10. 6.

'the more that people believed in the prodigies the more prodigies were announced' (*quae quo magis credebant simplices ac religiosi homines, eo plura nuntiabantur*). Take a part of one [1] of these lists (in 207 B.C.):

Before the Consuls went forth there was a nine-day sacrifice celebrated, because at Veii it had rained stones from heaven. And after one prodigious sight was once minded and spoken of, there were (as it is commonly seen) others also reported: namely, that in Minturnae the temple of Jupiter, and the sacred grove of Marcia were smitten with lightning; and at Atellae the wall and gate. The men of Minturnae spake also of a more fearful thing, to wit, that there ran a river of blood in their very gate. Last of all, at Capua [2] a wolf entered the gate at night, and worried and dismembered one of the watchmen.

These wonderful signs were expiated with sacrificing greater beasts, and a supplication was holden for one day, by virtue of a decree from the Pontiffs. . . . And men's minds were no sooner freed of one religious scruple, but they were troubled again with another. For word was brought, that at Frusino there was an infant born, as big as ordinary a child is at four years of age. And the thing was not so strange for bigness, as for that it was born doubtful, whether it were male or female. The wizards that were sent for out of Etruria said that this was a foul monster, and that it should be had forth of the dominion of Rome, and drowned in the deep, so as it might touch no ground. Whereupon they put it alive in a coffer, and when they had carried it a good way into the sea, they flung it in. Moreover the Pontiffs made a decree that certain virgins in three companies, nine apiece, should go through the city and sing certain canticles.

In one passage[3] Livy cannot conceal his scorn for 'the degraded superstition which thrusts the gods into connexion with the most trivial occurrence,' such as the fact that some mice had injured the gilding of a particular image; and yet immediately afterwards he points out that the subsequent defeat and death of Marcellus in that year (208) were, in the popular mind, connected with these same portents.

Of the various elements which were brought in to reinforce,

---

[1] Livy, XXVII, 37.
[2] By Capua now is meant only the shadow of what before 211 had been a great city; now there was only *tanquam urbs, aliqua aratorum sedes* (XXVI, 16. 7-8). The wolves had realised the difference.
[3] XXVII, 23. 4.

as men supposed, the waning power of the old city gods, the most conspicuous were the increased attention paid to Apollo,[1] and the worship of the Great Mother, who was supposed to be somehow contained in a meteoric stone which in 205 B.C. was brought with great pomp from Asia Minor and installed in a temple at Rome — all in accordance with instructions by the pontiffs. Of more private, though widespread, innovations, the worship of Bacchus, which thirty years later [2] we find all over Italy, is the most striking example. It is clear, as Dr. Warde Fowler has pointed out, that the old city religion never recovered from the shock of the war; and that, with this loosening of the bonds of primitive superstition, there began a more liberal attitude toward the idea of deity in general. It is natural to compare such effects with the new temper of which most of us are conscious here and now in many of our straiter forms of dogma or sect; for these in their turn have been shaken by the war of our own day. We all know how denominational barriers have shrunk and crumbled since 1914; and a learned friend of mine, who is wont to seek occasional diversion in the correspondence columns of what used to be called the evangelical weeklies, represented to me in a characteristic way the change of feeling which he noted. He had found, he said, a number of high authorities to be unanimous in the view that new instructions had been issued to St. Peter; in the case of those who fell in the war, at all events on the side of the Allies, passport formalities at the Golden Gate were completely suspended! The truth is that there are some kinds of dogma which may maintain themselves in ordinary times but which collapse under stress of some natural feeling strongly stirred in the whole community. Hard and fast doctrines about the future life, preached from scores of pulpits fifty years ago, suddenly broke like bubbles when every other home was mourning a father or a son.

Now it was far from an accident that the noble family, or group of noble families, which made the Scipionic circle and which was left by the war in a position of unmistakeable leader-

---

[1] The Ludi Apollinares were established in 212 B.C.

[2] See the *Senatus Consultum de Baccanalibus* of 186 B.C.; Livy, XXXIX, 8–19.

ship in Roman society, was also enthusiastic for Greek culture and with it for the study of Greek philosophy. After the Punic War we find the poet Ennius and (a little later) Terence, each in his own way devoted to the task of spreading Greek ideas, working under the protection of the Scipios; and a generation later Scipio Aemilianus, the friend of Polybius, was also closely associated with the famous Stoic, Panaetius.[1] Through the influence of this circle and of other men like-minded, there came into Rome, not merely the fresh current of Greek analysis and enquiry, steadily dissolving the older civic religion, but also the teachings of the most active Greek philosophy of the century, namely, Stoicism. And in Stoicism, as has so often been pointed out,[2] lay the main current of progress for the human spirit, a current which two centuries later was mingled in the deeper tide of Christianity. However distressing, therefore, the process of disillusion which began in the Punic War might and did appear to high-minded onlookers at the time, there can be no doubt that it contributed something to the humanising of Europe.

But if the calamities of the war, especially in its first three years, so deeply overthrew the old confidence of the Roman people, how was it recovered? What was it that in the end won them the victory over Hannibal, a greater general than any they had known? No one will suggest that it was the military prowess of any one man, deeply as they were indebted to the caution of Fabius and the more brilliant gifts of Scipio, to mention only these. Both great men failed seriously more than once; and neither of them could have had a chance of mending his country's fortunes but for the conditions through which they were chosen and by which in the long run they were supported. If the answer is to be put into a single phrase it can be only this — the victory was won by the genius and the character of the Roman people. It has not been quite fully realised how frequently in crises of the war individual judgement failed completely, but the popular instinct made a right

[1] Cicero, *Academica*, II, 2. 5.
[2] See Professor E. V. Arnold's *Stoicism at Rome*, p. 20, footnote, and Chapters 7 and 8, below.

decision. If ever a war was won by a nation and not by a single man, it was the war against Hannibal.

Take, for instance, the fundamental problem of finance. Judge from a single scene (in 215 B.C.) the way in which this part of the burden was borne:[1]

But as the number of them that paid taxes was greatly diminished by so great overthrows of the armies, so those few that remained, if they were to be burdened with exactions many times increased, would be plagued and ruined another way, therefore it was concluded that unless the Commonweal were supported by credit, she could not sustain herself by her own wealth. So it was agreed, that Fulvius the Praetor must assemble all the people together and declare unto them the necessity that the Commonweal was driven unto; and must exhort all them that had enriched themselves by taking the contracts issued by the State, that they should now make a present of a period of time to the Commonweal; for it was out of the Commonweal that they were grown to their present riches; and that they should undertake to furnish the army in Spain with all the supplies which it now needed, on condition that they be paid therefor first of all creditors out of the common chest, when it should be again stored with money. [Thus the Praetor made declaration of these matters in the open assembly of the people, and withal appointed a certain day, whereupon he minded to put forth the contracts for the soldiers' clothing and corn to be provided for the Spanish army, and all the other things now requisite for the fleet. When the day was come, there presented themselves unto him three companies of nineteen men, purposing to take these contracts, making only two requests, the one that while they were engaged in this public service, they should be exempt from service in the army; the other that whatsoever they shipped, should be transported at the risk of the Commonweal against all enemy force or violence of tempest. Both these requests being granted, they took upon them the matter, and so the Commonweal was served, by the money of private persons.

You will observe, there is no hint of any five per cent or six per cent interest to be paid on the sums they thus advanced. Patriotism had not become a profitable private investment.

Notice next a few cases of the wisdom shown by various commanders not of the first rank, men whose names scarcely appear in history at all.

[1] Livy, XXIII, 48. 9.

An incident (reminding one rather of our troubles with the "Black and Tans") in which the dangers of the use of irregular forces were happily forestalled is recorded of the year 210 B.C., when, by the capture of Agrigentum (following on that of Syracuse), the island of Sicily was finally reduced to peace. During the war the different communities of the island had taken different sides, and nearly every town had been fighting with its neighbour. The Roman governor, Laevinus by name, saw that it was urgently necessary to encourage these communities to resume their proper work of growing corn, and that not for their own sake merely, but to produce food for Rome. During the hostilities a band of nondescript ruffians, 4000 strong, most of whom, as Livy briefly puts it,[1] 'had committed capital crimes both when they lived in their own states and afterwards,' had been of some use on the Roman side; but their way of living, 'by brigandage and plunder,' was a thorn in the side of any peaceful community. Laevinus did not feel equal, while the war lasted, to the task of reforming their morals; but they must be got out of Sicily; so he put them all on shipboard and transported them to Rhegium, a Roman colony much distressed by the nearness of Hannibal's army and the hostility of the half-barbarous Bruttians all round them, who had taken Hannibal's side. The 4000 irregulars were likely, says Livy, to be 'very serviceable to the men of Rhegium, who needed a force used to brigandage' for harrying the land of the Bruttians.

In the year 208 B.C., when the doughty Marcellus was defeated and killed through his own imprudence in a reconnaissance,[2] his body came into Hannibal's possession. His colleague, Crispinus, also had received a serious wound in the engagement, from which he died a month or two later; but he had enough foresight to send round to all the neighbouring towns a warning that Marcellus was dead, and that Hannibal was in possession of his ring with its seal; and that therefore, if they received any letters purporting to be sealed by Marcellus, they might know at once that they were forged by Hannibal. So he brought it about that Hannibal suffered a

[1] XXVI, 40. 17.   [2] XXVII, 28.

considerable defeat instead of securing possession of the town of Salapia. In fact, he was forced to retreat to the southern extremity of Italy near Locri, whence he was afterwards able to emerge only for short spaces of time.

Perhaps the best example of soldierly judgement, in a commander on the second line, is the way in which a member of the great Sempronian family, an ancestor of the Gracchi, dealt with an army of what the Romans called volunteers; that is to say, of men who enlisted as slaves in the hope of earning their freedom. The enrolling of such men was always regarded as a desperate expedient, but after Cannae, age limits and all other limits had to go. Sempronius, after more than a year of training, decided to venture on a battle.

"Now," said Sempronius,[1] "the time has come of acquiring the liberty which so long you have hoped for. To-morrow you are to confront your enemies with banner displayed, and to fight in a plain and open ground, where without fear of any ambush, the trial may be made with valour. Whosoever therefore can bring me the head of an enemy, him my pleasure is to make free immediately: but whosoever giveth ground and turneth back, on him will I do justice as on a bond-slave.[2] Now every man hath his future condition lying in his own hands: for the promise is not mine only but that of Marcellus the consul, and ratified by all the Senate."

If we may accept the story as it stands (and there are reasons against supposing it to be a fiction), this somewhat primitive method of proving one's valour — to produce an enemy's head — turned out to be highly inconvenient. Sempronius soon corrected his mistake and ordered the heads of slain enemies to be left as they were; adding that if the battle was won, he would enfranchise his whole army without distinction.

But when they were returned laden with booty into the camp, they found there were almost 4000 of the voluntary soldiers who had fought but faintly, and had not broken into the enemy's camp with the rest; these for fear of punishment had seized a little hill not far from the camp, and there remained. But the morrow after, being brought away from thence by their commanders they arrived

---

[1] Livy, XXIV, 14. 6 (214 B.C.).   [2] That meant that he was to be crucified.

again at the camp, just when Gracchus had summoned his soldiers to an assembly. There, after Gracchus had first rewarded his old soldiers with military gifts each according to his good service in that battle, then, as concerning the slave-volunteers he said this much: that he had rather they were all commended by him, good and bad one with another, than that one of them that day should taste of any punishment: and therefore he pronounced them all free to the benefit, happiness, and felicity, both of the Commonweal, and of themselves. At this word, they lifted up their voices aloud with exceeding cheerfulness, first congratulating and embracing one another, then lifting their hands on high and praying of the gods all good blessings for the people of Rome, and especially for Gracchus. "Then," quoth Gracchus, "before I had made you all alike free, I would not set upon any of you, either the mark of a stout soldier, or that of a coward. But now I have discharged the promise made to you by the Commonweal, and for fear lest the difference between prowess and cowardice should be forgotten, I will take express order that the names of all of those, whose conscience accuses them of avoiding the hazard of battle, and who erewhile withdrew themselves apart, be brought to me; they shall be called forth every one by name, and I will compel them to take an oath that (unless it be for sickness) so long as they shall continue in soldiery, they will neither eat nor drink but standing upon their feet. And this punishment (I am sure) ye will willingly take in good part, if ye consider better of it and see that ye could not have had any lighter mark of shame for your cowardly service."

By this judicious (and humorous) compromise he strengthened the discipline of his army, and at the same time secured the gratitude of all the volunteers by fully discharging his pledge.

In some cases it was men of the rank and file merely whose loyalty or insight proved decisive. In 207 B.C. a foraging party of Roman privates caught a body of six horsemen (four Gauls and two Numidians), who were carrying the famous despatch from Hasdrubal announcing his arrival in Italy to his brother Hannibal. These foragers took their prisoners to their commander, who handled them straitly and got from them the despatch, which, without unsealing, he sent at once to the consul Claudius, who was in command in the south. This incident, as we know, was the real turning-point of the war, because it enabled Claudius to make his famous forced march to join his colleague Livius on the Metaurus, and with this doubled army to defeat Hasdrubal.

The most notable case of a private soldier's action was after the overwhelming defeat of the two older Scipios in Spain in the year 212.[1] Both commanders had fallen, and their armies were reduced to fragments. The survivors of one of the armies were collected by a young cavalry trooper called Marcius, who succeeded not only in fortifying a camp, but in uniting all the remnants of both armies. Chosen commander by the soldiers themselves, he inflicted a serious defeat on the Carthaginians, taking one of their camps and keeping the Roman cause safe until, in response to a despatch from him to the Senate, a new commander arrived.

But these individual achievements, however interesting, are less instructive than the cases in which the courage and wisdom of the community as a whole somehow prevailed over personal or partisan failings in their leaders.

In the year after Cannae, the first of the thirty tribes called on to vote for new consuls had nominated two men, of whom one was practically untried in the field and the other had been tried and proved to be more or less incompetent. Livy records a speech[2] in which the old Dictator, Fabius, talked to the people like a father, warning them that this was no time for experiments; they must choose the best consuls they can get; so the tribe humbly went back and voted again, and all the tribes followed its example in choosing now the Dictator himself as one of the two consuls. Incidentally we note the neglect of precedent by appointing to a consulship the man who was actually holding the election; but constitutional precedents in war time were things that the Romans knew how to deal with.

A more important case[3] in which the common goodwill prevailed over private bitterness was in the election of Livius in 208 B.C. for the consulship of the following year. Livius had been consul some years before, and, after the end of his office, had been accused before the people of some real or supposed breach of duty, and condemned to a fine. This he had taken bitterly to heart; he retired into private life far from Rome, and

---

[1] Livy, XXV, 37.   [2] XXIV, 8.   [3] XXVII, 34.

lived on his farm for eight years. His friends in the Senate had with difficulty persuaded him to come back, and now the majority of the Senate were eager that he should be made consul.

The only man in the whole city that opposed this, was Livius himself, to whom this dignity was being offered. He blamed the levity and inconstancy of the people: saying, that they had had no pity of him when it was needed, — namely, while he was in question and was wearing the garments proper to an accused man; but now against his will, they offered him the white robe of a candidate for the Consulship. Thus (quoth he) they punish, thus they honour the same persons. If they took me for a good and honest man, why condemned they me, as they did, for a guilty one? If they found me in fault, what cause have they to trust me with a second Consulship, who used the former so badly? As he argued in this wise, the Senate reproved him: "Like as the curstness and rigour of parents is to be mollified by patience on their children's part, even so the hard dealing of a man's country is to be mitigated by patience and sufferance."

So Livius gave way, and consented further, at the entreaty of the Senate, to lay aside during his term of office his old personal quarrel with his colleague Claudius.[1] The soundness of the people's judgement was signally vindicated by the victory which these two Consuls together won over Hasdrubal at the Metaurus in the following year. When one reads this story, and compares it with the sorry record of the committee [2] in 1915 which decided on the tragic adventure of Gallipoli, it is impossible not to wonder whether that calamity need have happened if the animosities of individual politicians and commanders could have been controlled by public opinion in England as they were in ancient Rome.

But perhaps the most striking case in which the popular instinct prevailed over personal jealousies was in the critical moment, in 205 B.C., when it was determined whether or not young Scipio Africanus, after six years spent in expelling the enemy from Spain, was to be allowed to cross into Africa to attack them at home. Scipio was determined to go, and he had let it be understood that, if the Senate failed to give him the

[1] Livy, XXVII, 34. 6.
[2] See the Blue Book Cd. 8490, *Report of the Royal Commission on the Dardanelles Expedition*, 1917.

commission, he meant to carry it over the Senate's head by a vote of the popular assembly. Such a precedent would have been a disaster to the Senate; in fact, it would have anticipated the fall of the constitution by nearly a century.

How was it settled?

The Tribunes of the people intervened with one of those transparent but useful pretences in which politicians take delight: the right thing is done; but done in such a way that to the defeated party is given the privilege of stating loudly that it has triumphed!

The Tribunes persuaded the Senate that it must give way; and they persuaded Scipio to leave the matter to the Senate. Scipio therefore withdrew his threat; but the result was that he was sent to govern Sicily, with permission to cross into Africa if he wished.

Lastly let me give you Livy's account of two examples of statesmanship not connected with the names of any individuals but springing straight from the instinct of the community. They concerned two difficulties strangely parallel to two which we also had to face. The first [1] is the way in which, in 209 B.C., the Romans handled what was practically a revolt of twelve out of their thirty colonies, that is, the communities of Latin citizens in different parts of Italy. Envoys from these twelve colonies complained bitterly of the length of time during which many of their citizens had been kept at the front, and flatly refused to supply any more men.

The Consuls, amazed at this unexpected turn, being desirous to deter the disaffected colonies from so detestable a resolution, supposed they would prevail more by chastising and rebuke, than by gentle dealing: and therefore they replied to the deputies that they had presumed to say unto the Consuls what the Consuls could not find in their hearts to deliver in the Senate House. For this was not a mere refusal of war-service but no better than an open revolt from the people of Rome. Therefore they were best to return again speedily into their several colonies, and consult with their neighbours and countrymen, as though nothing at all had been said. . . . When the Consuls had dealt with them a long time in this manner, the envoys, nothing moved with their words, made answer

[1] Livy, XXVII, 9. 8.

again, that neither they knew what message to take home; nor would their town-councils know what new resolution to take; since they had not any more men to be mustered for soldiers, nor money to provide for their pay. The Consuls seeing them so stiffly and obstinately bent, made report thereof to the Senate. Whereupon every man was stricken into so great trouble of mind, that many of them declared that the empire of Rome was come to an end. The like, said they, the rest of the Colonies will do: all our confederates and allies are combined to betray the city of Rome unto Hannibal. But the Consuls comforted the Senate, and bade them be of good cheer, saying, that all the other eighteen colonies would continue loyal and fast in their duty. . . . Upon the aid [1] of these eighteen colonies, the Roman state at this time rested and stood; and these all were highly thanked both in the Senate, and in the assembly of the people. As for the other twelve colonies which had refused to do their obedience, the Senate gave express command that they should not be so much as once named: and that the Consuls should neither give them their dispatch, nor retain them, nor so much as speak unto them. This silent kind of rebuke without word-giving, seemed to suit best with the majesty of the people of Rome.

Afterwards, in 204 B.C., they were punished; each town was ordered to provide a contingent twice the size of the largest that it had ever sent, and these to be taken from their wealthiest citizens and to be sent on foreign service. The colonies declared this impossible, but soon found it wise to obey.[2]

The second case is the treatment given to a large body of men — some 10,000 to start with, and in the end considerably more — who were known as the 'Soldiers of Cannae,' that is, the men who ran away from the great battle and afterwards, by one road and another, drifted back to this or that Roman force. By the end of the year 216, they were all under the command of Marcellus. Their history as a body precisely covers the period with which we have been concerned, from 215 to 203, and nothing could be more characteristic of the Roman attitude to the war. We all know that this problem, though it was rarely mentioned in public reports, was one which a great number of our own company commanders, and even brigadiers, if not divisional officers, had to face at different moments of the war on the Western front; and I sup-

[1] Livy, XXVII, 10. 9.   [2] XXIX, 15.

pose that the instinct of an English general was to distribute as widely as possible among his different units the men who had shown themselves unreliable, so as to abolish, as far as possible, any corporate traditions of slackness which might have contributed to their plight. The last thing, I fancy, that would occur to an English commander would be to form them up in a corps by themselves, and he would not dream of keeping them for twelve years outside the fighting zone.

Now note briefly what happened in Italy in 216 B.C. A few months after the disaster of Cannae, the Romans had lost 25,000 men (that is, the whole of two legions, with their contingents of allies) in another overwhelming defeat in the north of Italy by the Gauls, who had lured the Roman commander into the midst of a forest which they had then literally brought down upon his head. They overturned on to the advancing legions a crushing weight of trees, whose trunks had been carefully sawn through beforehand, for a great distance on either side of the track. Yet this tragical addition to their losses did not make the Senate less zealous for the quality of the Roman forces. On the contrary, directly after this, they gave instructions to Marcellus to weed out carefully from his force all soldiers who had had any share in the rout at Cannae; and to the number of 10,000 they were transported to Sicily, with the grim instructions that they were to serve there without pay, on menial duties only, and with no leave of absence until the army of Hannibal should have left Italy. So there they sailed, a disgraced and dejected multitude; two years later their numbers were increased from a curious source. In 214 B.C. the Censors drew up a list of all the men of military age in Rome (they proved to be over 2000 in number) who had had no official exemption from military service but who had not offered themselves for service since the beginning of the war. They were bundled out of Rome and sent to join the soldiers of Cannae in Sicily under the same conditions. Not exactly an encouraging (or even welcome) set of newcomers! In 209 B.C. the number was increased by the addition of the survivors of a serious defeat suffered at Herdonea — many hundreds more dumped upon this human dust-heap.

What was the effect of this treatment on the minds of these men? That question is naturally put by anyone who has thought at all (and which of us has not?) on the problem of our own disaffected citizens; for that is the name by which I should describe the Conscientious Objectors, though I do not wish by the word disaffected to imply any general and indiscriminate condemnation. Their minds may have been set — in some cases they certainly were set — on what they thought a higher allegiance than that toward the country which fed, clothed, and defended them at the cost of the lives of their fellow citizens; but toward that country they were certainly disaffected; and we all know what a burden they were to the government and to the rest of our community in the struggle in which we were engaged. The Roman treatment of this kind of people, stern as it was, shows none of the persecutor's temper: they were protected from any outburst of popular anger; they were fed, and clothed, and sent away to what was then a distant region, — no postal service ran then between Rome and Sicily, — in a place where they could be put to useful work, but in no position of danger, or of trust which they could betray. Now what was the effect on the minds of these men? In the light of our own experience one of the most interesting passages in the whole of Livy is the speech which he puts [1] into the mouth of a deputation from this body of men to the Proconsul, Marcellus, when he was in charge of Sicily in the year 213 B.C., a year later than the arrival of the shirkers from Rome.

"We, against whom nothing can be objected at all, unless it be this, that we were the cause that at least some citizens of Rome might be said to remain alive of all those that were at the battle of Cannae: we, I say, are sent far enough off, not only from our homes and from Italy, but also from all enemies, while we wax old in exile, to the end that we should have no hope or opportunity to cancel our disgrace, to mitigate the anger of our fellow-citizens, and finally to die with honour. But it is neither end of shame nor reward of valour, that we now crave: only that we might be permitted to make proof of our courage. Pains and perils we seek for, and to be employed in dangerous adventures, like men and soldiers. Two

[1] Livy, XXV, 6. 17.

years already there hath been sharp and hot war in Sicily. . . .
The shouts of them that fight, the very clattering and ringing of
their armour we can hear where we are; and we sit still and idly do
nothing, as if we had neither hands nor weapons to fight with. Will
you yourself, oh Marcellus, make trial of us, and of our valour, by
sea, by land, in pitched field, or in making assault on walled townes?
Put us to it, and spare not. . . ."

With these words they fell down prostrate at Marcellus' feet.
Marcellus answered them that he had neither power of himself, nor
instructions otherwise, to satisfy their request. Howbeit, write he
would to the Senate; and according as the Senate should give direction, so he would do.

You see they did not venture to ask for payment or recall,
or for any privilege but that of being allowed to fight. Their
grievance was that the war was going on almost within their
hearing, but they were never trusted with swords in their
hands. What did the Senate reply?

That as concerning those soldiers, who had forsaken their fellows
fighting before Cannae, the Senate saw no reason why they should
be put in trust any more with the affairs of the Commonwealth;
but if M. Claudius Marcellus the proconsul thought it good otherwise, he might do according to that which he judged convenient,
and to stand with his own credit and the safety of the State. Provided always, that not one of them be dispensed with, nor freed
from service, nor rewarded with any military gift in token of valour:
nor yet returned home again into Italy, so long as the enemy made
abode there.

It seems that, from this time, they were occasionally employed on real military duty; but they were still maintained as
a totally separate corps, not mixed with the other armies in
Sicily; and four years later, after they had been joined by the
runaways from Herdonea, we find a renewal of severity toward a certain class, namely, the wealthier of them who
served in the cavalry.[1] The rest, however, enjoyed a more or
less legitimised position; they were still kept separate from
other troops, but were assigned year by year by the Senate as
part of the forces entrusted to the officer in command of Sicily.
This continued until 204 B.C., when the whole situation was
changed by the arrival of Scipio. We have just seen how he

[1] Livy, XXVII, 11. 4.

had secured, after a struggle, the command of Sicily with permission to cross to Africa if he chose. But beyond the forces in Sicily no army had been given him for the purpose, and like another brilliant Italian commander of a later day, Garibaldi, Scipio had to rely for his great enterprise largely on the help of volunteers. Naturally he was not inclined to despise any trained forces that he could secure; and having received a favourable report from his predecessors of the way in which these patient men of Cannae had behaved in small operations in the last six years, he proclaimed that he would make no difference between the men of this group and the others in choosing men for the invasion of Africa. After weeding out the physically unfit, he embodied the rest in his army, and they shared in the final victory of Zama. The Romans conquered even Hannibal in the field because they had first achieved a victory over the spirit of disaffection in the hearts of their own citizens. How far can we be sure that we did the same?

VII

THE PHILOSOPHY OF VERGIL [1]

ONE of the most distinguished of living British philosophers
once declared that the best thing which any system of meta-
physics could hope to do was to suggest a new point of view.
At the moment he was lecturing on the mysterious Hegel;
and though it was twenty-five years ago, I still remember the
feeling of relief which the declaration produced. Here was a
profound student of Hegel, no mean author himself of metaphysical theory, deliberately acknowledging that no philosophic system, however brilliant, could hope to be literally
true; he was content if we recognised that all great systems
provided new and fruitful points of view from which the world
could be studied. Somewhat in this spirit, even those who
have no claim to be philosophers may still, perhaps, discern
something in a great poet which it is not unreasonable to describe as a philosophy, pervading his mature work. It certainly does not amount to a metaphysical system; but it does
seem to open to us a rather striking point of view. All lovers
of Vergil know the lines in Tennyson's address to him, and we
all recognise their truth:

> Thou that seest universal Nature moved by universal mind,
> Thou majestic in thy sadness at the doubtful doom of human kind.

Behind and beneath these two conceptions which Tennyson
ascribes to Vergil, there was a certain mental attitude which I
should like to make clear, if I can. The theory is submitted to
criticism with some diffidence, yet in the conviction that it is
at least true so far as it goes, and that it unites and explains

[1] This lecture was first put together for the John Rylands Library on November
10, 1920, and published, as then given, in the *John Rylands Library Bulletin* (January, 1922). In that shape it was delivered to the meetings of several Branches of
the Classical Association in England; but it is here printed in the greatly revised
form in which it was presented at Harvard and elsewhere in the United States in
the spring of 1927.

many features in Vergil's work, both in his style and in his thought.

The attitude which we are to study is that which I believe Vergil to have held in the maturity of his powers, that is, in the part of his life occupied in writing the *Georgics* and the *Aeneid*. Nothing, therefore, need be said here about the sympathy with Epicurean teaching which, as we all know, marked Vergil's youth.[1] On the other hand, his relation to Stoicism will naturally come into view.

Let me begin by remarking a general fact about Vergil which is too little realised. We are apt to regard him merely as what he became, the truest and most complete representative known to us of Roman life. Yet when we compare him with the writers of his own day and of the preceding generation, I think it is true to say that in one respect he stands apart from them all, namely, in the depth of his knowledge of Greek writers, and in the eagerness with which he seeks to infuse his own account of things Roman and Italian with a spirit drawn directly from Greek sources. A simple example is the deliberate way in which (to the confusion of some modern critics) he has continually coupled Greek and Italian folk-lore in the *Georgics*. At the outset [2] the Greek wood nymphs, the Dryads, are invited, in a manner which shocked that most respectable of commentators, John Conington, to join the dance of purely Italian deities, the Fauns; and Pan, the Greek god of the Arcadian hills, is to come and take part with Minerva and Silvanus, both Italian gods. So in the charming passage describing the farmers' festival,[3] Italian fashions, like those of the sacred masks (*oscilla*) hung on fruit trees to swing with the wind, appear side by side with Greek rites in the worship of Bacchus associated with the Greek drama. So at the outset of Book II, Bacchus is invoked to help Vergil sing of the tendance of vines, but not without being bidden to lay aside his buskins — that is, to turn from the tragedies which were celebrated in his honour at Athens and come to inspire a not less

[1] See "The Youth of Vergil," in *Great Inheritance*, chap. 4, esp. pp. 100 ff.
[2] *Georg.*, I, 11 ff.
[3] *Ibid.*, II, 380–396.

worthy subject with not less poetic power. I need hardly even remind you of the countless passages in the *Aeneid* where Vergil has adapted to his purpose some incident or utterance of Greek poetry. Let me rather ask your attention to one or two more general characteristics of his point of view.

There were deeply imprinted on Vergil's mind some of the most typical of all Greek habits of thought. The late Mr. Alfred W. Benn, in his final and brilliant survey of *The Philosophy of Greece*,[1] pointed out two features, closely related, which appear in almost all Greek systems of philosophy. One was the dread of extremes, a faith in that most national of all Greek virtues which they called σωφροσύνη, a word which we variously — and always unsuccessfully — translate by 'temperance,' 'moderation,' 'self-control,' 'sanity,' 'sound-mindedness'; that central firmness and serenity of character which preserves men from being the victims of sudden passion in the world of action, or of wild extremes of belief in the world of thought.

The second characteristic, which seems at first less interesting, was the habit of antithesis, of considering things in pairs, such as heat and cold, darkness and light. This in the Greek language is well represented by the humble and everyday particles which, on the threshold of his acquaintance with Greek writers, the schoolboy finds so hard to represent, the simple μέν and δέ — 'on the one hand,' 'on the other hand,' as he laboriously renders them. I suppose no one ever began to read, say, the speeches of Thucydides without wishing that the Greek affection for these particles had been less pronounced. Yet if we turn to the writings of the tutor of Thucydides, the rhetorician Antiphon, and see how every page is studded with these antithetic points, we realise that Thucydides, even in his most argumentative moments, was probably less given to antithesis for its own sake than were most Greek speakers in the years of his boyhood.

But what, it will be asked, has this rather quaint peculiarity of Greek diction to do with such serious things as those of which philosophy treats? The answer is simple, namely, that

[1] London, 1908.

in almost all Greek philosophers there is an implicit dualism of some kind or other: for example, the contrast in Plato between the invisible, real, existing Ideas and the imperfect copies or approximations to them which made up for him the visible world; or in Aristotle's *Ethics*, the conception of every virtue as the middle term between two extremes, the virtue of courage, for example, being the middle point between the extremes of cowardice on the one hand and rashness on the other. In earlier systems we recall the Mind which Anaxagoras conceived as imposing order on Chaos; or the two principles of Love and Strife, centripetal and centrifugal forces, which Empedocles regarded as governing the physical as well as the human world. These examples will be enough to show that the characteristic Greek habit of thinking and speaking in antithesis was not merely a trick of words, but corresponded to something quite substantial in the Greek view of things. Most of us who have any interest in philosophy know how striking and impressive a revival was given to this kind of antithesising by the speculations of Hegel, with his fundamental proposition that everything implies and generates its opposite.

To these two characteristics of the Greek temper we may add a third which everyone will recognise, a certain childlike capacity for wonder — a standing readiness for new experiment, the virtue of perpetual hope and youth in the sphere of thought. This was the most engaging thing about Socrates, and Socrates in this was a most typical Greek. There was no problem which he was not prepared to discuss, in the hope that careful study of its conditions might reveal new light; and the same refreshing candour in discussing first principles meets us on every page of Greek tragedy. It is not quite identical, and yet it has some kinship, with the adventurous spirit which to European eyes is so marked a feature of American life. In Homer, though it is not common in the political sphere, it is very marked in Odysseus, and lies indeed almost at the root of his character. So Dante saw in that famous Twenty-sixth Canto of the *Inferno*, which represents Odysseus as meeting his end through continually pressing forward to explore new tracts of ocean; an attitude which Tennyson's *Ulysses* has made familiar to English readers.

Now I think it may be maintained that all these three characteristics of the Greek spirit are more deeply marked in Vergil than in any other Roman: first, the reverence for self-control; second, the habit of wonder, or intellectual curiosity; and third, the method of looking at things from a dual, antithetic standpoint.

On the first, Vergil's hatred of extremes, and love of self-control, I need say little. It was shared, as we all know, by his intimate friend Horace, though perhaps the Golden Mean, which Horace so faithfully celebrates, did not signify quite all that Vergil meant by *servare modum* [1] ('keeping the limit'). We need only recall, in passing, the contrast on which the whole story of the *Aeneid* is based: that Aeneas does learn to practise self-control, to sacrifice his own private hopes and desires to the call of duty, even in the hardest case, where it bade him abandon his love for Dido, whereas his brilliant rival, Turnus, never will make the sacrifice. He is *violentus* from first to last, passionate, reckless, and contemptuous of any law or promise that would interfere with his wild, impulsive will. For example, he broke through the fixed custom of what the ancient world counted honourable warfare by stripping the armour from the body of the lad Pallas, whom he had slain, and making it his own instead of dedicating it to a god; and he persisted in his suit for Lavinia's hand in defiance both of her father and of what he himself knew and in the end confessed [2] to be the command of Heaven.

Nor, again, need we stay to note examples of the eager, childlike wonder, merged in a deeper sense of mystery, [3] which was constantly in Vergil's mind as he looked upon the world. The only remark that need here be added on these two characteristics is this: that they may be both regarded as connected with the third, namely, the habit of looking at things from antithetic standpoints. For the self-control which the Greeks loved is a compromise in practice between contrasted motives

---

[1] *Aen.*, X, 502.   [2] VII, 423; XII, 27, with 895 and 931.
[3] On this, see *Great Inheritance*, pp. 35 ff.; and p. 147, below.

of action; and the mysticism, which is a continual sense of wonder unsolved, may be regarded as a kind of spiritual compromise between contrasted views of the truth.

It is the third point which I am now mainly concerned to examine — Vergil's antithetic or dualistic habit of mind. It is so characteristic of his thought that it has left a marked impress on his style; and it may well be that, when it is once stated, it may seem so commonplace a matter as hardly to deserve a name, much less to be discussed at length. If you do so recognise it, and admit its reality, I shall be only too pleased. But then I must ask you to add it to the characteristics of Vergil's poetry which it is desirable for all Vergil's readers to understand; for, unless I am greatly mistaken, you will not find it stated in any of the commentaries.

Vergil was rarely content to see a fact, or a feeling, or an event, in which he was interested, as something which stood by itself. He instinctively sought for some parallel event, some complementary fact, to set beside the first. We may dismiss briefly one large group of these pairs, though it is characteristic of his narrative — the cases where the second fact involves no particular contrast, only a re-inforcement of the original statement: such as *Italiam Lavinaque litora* ('Italy and the Lavinian shore') at the outset of the *Aeneid;* or, in the same Book, where Dido promises,

> auxilio tutos dimittam opibusque iuuabo

('I will let you go protected by my support and aid you with my resources'), where the tongue-tied English schoolboy can think only of the one word 'help' to translate three of the four Latin words. It resembles very strongly the habit of parallel statement in Hebrew poetry, so familiar to us in the Psalms (*He hath founded it upon the seas and stablished it upon the floods*); and in this some scholars see evidence of a direct acquaintance on Vergil's part with some of the Jewish scriptures. Be that as it may, this dualism of mere confirmation is not what I am concerned to examine now; as my friend, Professor J. S. Mackenzie, points out to me, one can hardly be sure of more than this about it, that it is a way of dwelling on a particular thought natural to reflective minds.

But there is an interesting set of cases on which something must be said, though I should myself refer them to the same class of confirmatory repetition. In all of them Vergil mentions a n a t u r a l cause for some event side by side with a d i v i n e cause; and he often gives us to understand that both causes are true; so that, if we are to give a name to this view of causation, we must call it, not "supernatural," but rather "internatural." Sometimes, it is true, the alternatives are put in the form of a question, as when Nisus discloses to Euryalus his daring project of leaving the Trojan camp by night and making his way through the enemy's forces, in order to take word of their danger to Aeneas. He asks Euryalus: 'Is it the gods who inspire us with the ardour I feel, or does each of us make his own fatal desire into a god?' [1]   Where the parallel is put in the shape of a question, especially in the form 'by chance or by Heaven's will' (a form which is older than Vergil, as Professor William Greene justly points out [2]), Vergil may mean to express real doubt, a perplexity he cannot solve. A similar case is the ambiguous fate of Creusa,[3] 'snatched away by fate, or missing her way, or stopping in weariness.' But I have noted well over a score of examples where the identification is positive and complete, though only a few can be described here. The plainest and most explicit case is in the Fall of Troy in Book II of the *Aeneid*,[4] where Aeneas has his eyes opened by Venus, so that, instead of walls and houses crumbling in fire or before the assaults of the Greeks, — as he had supposed, — he now sees the hostile deities actually at work, Pallas with her thunder-cloud and Gorgon shield, Neptune with his trident, themselves crushing the doomed city into dust. So in the Fourth Book of the *Georgics* [5] Vergil asks in the same breath what god invented a particular art (namely, that of breeding bees) and then, 'whence did men's new experience take its rise,' implying that both inspiration and experience contributed. In the battle in the Tenth Book of the *Aeneid*,[6] Aeneas only just escapes destruction from a band of seven brothers, who are all

[1] *Aen.*, IX, 184.
[2] *American Journal of Philology*, XLIII (1922), 344.
[3] *Aen.*, II, 738–739. Similarly, III, 262; X, 109–110.
[4] II, 603–616.   [5] IV, 315–316.   [6] X, 331.

attacking him at once, because 'some of their darts are beaten
back from his shield and helmet' and 'some are turned aside
from grazing him by his divine mother.' In the same Book,[1]
the reader wonders why the two young warriors, Pallas and
Lausus, never meet in conflict, and Vergil gives two reasons:
first, that their supporters on each side crowd up so thickly
that neither hands nor weapons can be used; and then (four
lines farther on), that 'the ruler of great Olympus has forbid-
den them to meet.' At the end of the Eleventh Book [2] we
learn that Turnus deserts the ambush which he has laid for
Aeneas, in anger at the news of the death of Camilla. But
Vergil adds, 'and so the cruel will of Jove demanded.' So in
the taunt which Remulus levels at the beleaguered Trojans:
'What god, what madness, drove you to Italy?'[3] In the
Second Book [4] the cause of the fall of Troy is given doubly:
'the fates of the gods and the Trojans' own minds' were
both bent to destruction. Destiny had decreed that Troy
must fall; the Trojans fulfilled this destiny by their cowardice in
leaving Laocoön to perish unaided (their panic is four times [5]
mentioned), and by interpreting his death as due to his wicked
daring, not to their own folly; they would not see the signs
of warning.

Above all, in the crowning scene of the defeat of Turnus, at
the end of the poem, the action of fate, in the shape of the
small bird sent by Jove, which Turnus takes (rightly, as we are
given to understand) for an evil omen,[6] is put side by side
with the inward reproach [7] of Turnus's own conscience, which
he avows after he has fallen. 'I deserve it, I confess,' are his
first words then. The two causes are almost explicitly identified in the lines in which Vergil tells us, first, that the 'dread
goddess' (that is, the little bird by which Turnus is daunted)
'denies him success wherever his valour seeks it'; and then,
that 'his breast is full of conflicting thoughts, he glances

---

[1] *Aen.*, X, 433.   [2] XI, 901.   [3] IX, 601.

[4] II, 54. Observe that the meaning of *mens* (*i. e., mens Troianorum*) is quite
clearly fixed by the fact that the half-line (*si mens non laeua fuisset*) is borrowed
from Eclogue I, 16, where it must mean 'if I had not been blind to the warning.'

[5] II, 200, 212, 228, 244.

[6] XII, 862–868.   [7] XII, 894–895 and 931.

toward the city, hesitates, and then turns to cast his dart, and cannot decide whether to fly or to attack.' [1]

This frequent suggestion,[2] that the will of Heaven is, after all, carried out by the action of human beings stirred by motives which they think to be their own, is characteristic of Vergil's treatment of the whole idea of Providence, and shows some affinity with the Stoic doctrine of the identity of Jove and Fate.[3] But from our present point of view it is only a conspicuous illustration of Vergil's habit of regarding the same thing from more than one standpoint.

But take now a more sharply cut type of this dualism, where the two points of view are not identical or even parallel, but definitely contrasted and hostile, so that we feel a certain surprise and are conscious, not of two parts of a single fact, but apparently of two conflicting, if not quite contradictory, experiences. In a word, Vergil seems to strike two notes which make, not a harmony, but a discord. The result is an incongruity which is either amusing or pathetic or both; and sometimes we cannot tell whether humour or pathos is uppermost. Take first an absolutely simple example, so simple that perhaps it may seem almost childish to dwell on it. Among other instructions to the bee-keeper for choosing a place for his beehive, Vergil warns him that it must not be near the nests of swallows. Why? Because they will carry off the bees to feed their young. Now how does Vergil describe this annoying procedure on the part of the swallows?

ore ferunt dulcem nidis immitibus escam.[4]

---

[1] *Aen.*, XII, 913–917.

[2] Other examples of precisely the same kind may be identified in *Aen.*, I, 382, 603, 709 with 710; II, 34, 336; III, 150 with 172, 331 with 332; IV, 352 with 354, 696; VI, 190 with 193; IX, 254, 744; XI, 118; XII, 222 with 228, 554 with 560. And the number may certainly be increased.

[3] Compare Professor E. V. Arnold's remark, in *Roman Stoicism* (Cambridge, 1911), p. 390: "Vergil, however, appears truly to hold the Stoic principle that Fate and Jove are one; he thus takes us at once to the final problem of philosophy, the reconciliation of the conceptions of law formed on the one hand by observing facts (the modern "Laws of Nature"), and on the other hand by recognising the moral instinct (the modern "Moral Law"). Vergil shows us how they may be, in practice, reconciled by a certain attitude of mind; and that attitude is one of resignation to, and coöperation with, the supreme power."

[4] *Georg.*, IV, 17.

Now I venture to think that no other Latin poet, and perhaps no other poet that I can name, of any nation, would have worded this statement in quite that way. It would have been natural for him, one thinks, to write *facilem* instead of *dulcem* — 'an easy prey for their cruel nestlings.' That would have enforced the point, namely, the greediness of the baby swallows and the consequent danger to the bees. But it may be objected that *dulcem* for this purpose is just as good as *facilem*: 'a sweet morsel' is just as likely to tempt the swallows as an 'easily captured' one. True; but what has Vergil done by choosing *dulcem?* We shall see at once, if for the word *immitibus* we substitute a more common epithet of young birds, say, *crepitantibus* ('twittering, clamorous'). What should we have then? 'A sweet morsel for their clamouring [that is, hungry] young.' If Vergil had written that, you would have seen clearly that he was expressing sympathy with the swallows and that he had forgotten to be sorry for the bees. But by using both the word *dulcem* and the word *immitibus* — 'a sweet morsel for their cruel nestlings' — Vergil expresses his sympathy, first with the swallows and then with the bees, in one and the same line, much to the schoolboy's perplexity. He does the same thing in the passage where he exhorts the farmer to clear away the long-standing wood and make the land subject to the plough.[1] What is the result? The 'newly conquered land gleams with the sheen of the ploughshare'; but the birds have had to leave their ancient homes and fly aloft, deserting their young. There is no doubt of Vergil's meaning. This is the farmer's duty; but all the same it is a tragedy for the birds.

So where Vergil is telling the farmer to dip his sheep again and again in the health-giving river (*fluvio mersare salubri*),[2] how does he describe the sheep who are to be dipped? They are the 'bleating creatures' (*balantum gregem*); and the two contrasted words, *balantum* and *salubri*, bring before us the whole scene — the terror of the sheep at being seized and dragged to the pool, and the noise they make when the turn of each comes. The epithet 'bleating' suddenly gives us the

---

[1] *Georg.*, II, 207–211.   [2] *Ibid.*, I, 272.

sheep's point of view instead of the shepherd's, and gives it, of course, with a smile, caught up at once by the word *salubri*, which shows how benevolent the shepherds are, whatever the sheep may think.

In all these cases Vergil practises a kind of brief quotation, a sort of suppressed "oratio obliqua." He describes part of the scene for a moment, as it appeared to the eyes of one of the actors in it. It is this which makes the story of the competitors in the Games in Book V so fresh and full of life; every one of them, in this way or that, is somehow allowed to present his own case; and we follow the rising and falling fortunes of each with a lively sympathy, as much for those who fail as for those who win.

In the story of the *Aeneid* the action is continually shared by two leading characters at a time, each presented to us with almost equal sympathy. Illustration is really needless. The most conspicuous example is that of Dido—with whom Vergil's sympathy is so clear that people often forget that he sympathised with Aeneas, too.[1] But we may glance at a less-known, though quite typical, scene — that between Juno and Venus in the celestial debate in Book X. The Book opens upon an assembly of the gods which has been summoned by Jove, who hopes to persuade the rival partisans to come to an agreement and so to end the war in Latium. When Jove has stated the situation and mildly deprecated their quarrel, Venus breaks in with a long plea on behalf of the Trojans, appealing to the oracles of fate which had been so often declared to Aeneas. Why, she asks, has Jove permitted the resistance of the Latins? Why are they allowed to attack the camp just when Aeneas has gone to seek help from Evander? Why must her dear Trojans be for ever in danger? The plea, like most of the speeches of Venus, is pathetic and ingenious rather than forceful; and it is not without covert allusions to Juno as the source of the mischief, though Juno is not expressly named, but only described as 'she' — the guilty 'she' who had sent Iris from the clouds to encourage Turnus to fight, and raised the Fury Allecto from hell to incite the Latins. By this complaint

[1] See p. 67, above, and *Great Inheritance*, chap. 6.

Juno is roused [1] to great anger and replies fiercely and directly to Venus, altogether forgetting to address the Chair.

After pointing out that Aeneas had gone away and left the camp of his own choice, Juno takes the offensive:

> Dost thou count it crime
> If Latin hands gird yon new Troy with flames,
> Or Turnus fight to save his fatherland?
> What censure hast thou then for Trojan hordes
> Seizing Italian fields and driving cattle,
> And flinging deadly brands on Latin towns?
> Choosing new kin, they drag affianced brides
> From lawful husbands; send their messengers
> To pray for peace, but line their prows with arms.
> Why troublest thou a city big with wars,
> Stirring fierce hearts?

Then Juno turns to ancient history:

> Was I concerned to sink
> Your fallen fortunes deeper in the dust?
> I? or the man who threw unhappy Troy
> Into Greek hands to spoil? Where lay the guilt
> That mingled continent with continent
> In war and broke their treaties by a theft?
> Did I take Paris into Spartan homes?
> Did I breed war and give it love for food?
> 'Twas then thou shouldst have taken thought to save
> Thy darlings; now too late thy anger flames,
> In taunts that lost their meaning long ago.

This eloquent protest did not convince Jupiter, who is merely grieved at the continued hostility of the goddesses, and dismisses the assembly. But Juno's speech has had at least one success; it has deceived no less a critic than Professor Saintsbury into believing its rhetorical statement about Lavinia (where Juno speaks of 'dragging brides from their lawful husbands'), as if it really corresponded to the facts, instead of being a partisan misrepresentation. Lavinia, of course, was never betrothed to Turnus, but was solemnly betrothed to Aeneas. We will not, therefore, follow Professor Saintsbury quite so far; but we may at least agree that the case against Aeneas and the Trojans is vigorously and sympathetically presented.

[1] *Aen.*, X, 62–95.

Observe further that this dramatic habit of Vergil's mind, his way of quickly changing from the point of view of one character to that of another, often gives an undertone of humour to the story. Even in the Sixth Book a certain grim incongruity colours the picture of old Charon, with his soiled raiment and unkempt hair, but with the green and fresh old age — of what? Of a god.[1] Or of the Sibyl, who has always a threat upon her lips but a concession in her heart. And there is one line in the *Aeneid* which amounts to direct and bitter satire; satire of a kind which, if it had occurred in a Christian poet, would have been regarded as something like blasphemy. In the Twelfth Book, who is the leader of the Latins who persuades them to refuse to let Turnus fight in single combat, and who thus makes them break the truce to which their king has solemnly sworn? It is the augur, Tolumnius. He had seen what he took for a portent: a flock of swans forcing an eagle to release one of their number whom it was carrying off. This the swans did by flying above the eagle [2] and pressing him down by sheer weight of numbers. Tolumnius cries out with pious exultation, 'This, this is what I have prayed for again and again; I recognise and accept Heaven's answer [*accipio agnoscoque deos*]. Follow me, ye Latins, and grasp your swords.' And he goes on to promise them, in virtue of his sacred authority, that the wicked invader, namely, Aeneas, shall be routed by their united effort, just as the eagle has been routed by the troop of swans. What is the sequel? When the battle has begun Tolumnius himself is slain.[3] Such was the answer to his prayer.

We must not leave altogether unmentioned the strange case of the young Ascanius. Somehow Vergil never seems to mention him without a smile. Think of him first in the sack of Troy, while his parents are weeping because his grandfather will not leave their home to escape the approaching flames; the child, of course, is quite unconscious of the trouble. But it is on him that the miraculous sign appears, 'a harmless halo of flame plays upon his curls.'[4] His anxious parents try to extinguish the flame by pouring water on it; but the old Anchises

---

[1] *Aen.*, VI, 304.   [2] XII, 259.   [3] XII, 461.   [4] II, 683.

recognises it as an omen and prepares to depart. Later on, when Aeneas is carrying his father on his back and his wife follows behind, the little Ascanius holds his hand, keeping up, adds the poet, 'with unequal steps' (*non passibus aequis*).[1] I wonder how many other poets, in describing such a scene, would have found room to mention the child's baby steps. Wordsworth, you will say; but then perhaps Wordsworth might have omitted to mention anything else! Again, when Dido and Aeneas ride out to their fateful hunt in the woods,[2] each attended by stately troops of followers, it is clear that the one person in the whole multitude who is full of pure delight is the boy Ascanius, 'riding on a swift horse, leaving behind now one band of comrades, now another, and longing that he may have [not mere stags to hunt but] some foaming boar or tawny lion from the Libyan hills'; his bright figure is like a gleam of sunshine across a lurid sky. Or, again, take the scene in Book V,[3] when the desponding old ladies of the Trojan host in Sicily have been evilly inspired to set fire to the ships, in order to put an end to their wanderings. News is brought to the warriors, who are absorbed in the Games, and Ascanius at once breaks away from his own part in them and rides off at full speed to the beach, greatly to the dismay of his tutors. 'Why, you must be mad,' he cries, 'my poor ladies [*heu! miserae ciues*]; what can you be expecting? This is not the camp of the enemy, it is your own hopes that you are giving to the flames. See, I am your own Ascanius'; and, like a boy, he pulls his helmet off and dashes it down on the ground before them, so that they may see at once who it is. There is an echo of the same delicate humour wherever Ascanius appears in the later Books.

In these cases the reader's sense of incongruity is aroused because the point of view of the narrator is changed. In the first case, the point of view shifts suddenly from the thoughts of the anxious parents, with their pail of cold water, to the insight of Anchises, who realises what the portent means. In the second example, we pass from the absorbing anxiety of Aeneas in burning Troy, to his feeling seven years after in retrospect,

---

[1] *Aen.*, II, 723. [2] IV, 156–159. [3] V, 671.

when he realises the picture of little Ascanius trotting by his side, unconscious of the danger, only thinking perhaps that his father is walking rather fast.[1]

But does all this, it may be asked, illustrate anything more than a habit of Vergil's imagination, lively enough, and perhaps characteristic? What has it to do with philosophy in any shape? And after all, why be concerned to ask about Vergil's philosophy at all, when, in the revelation which he gives us through the lips of Anchises in the Sixth Book, he declares explicitly the truth of a large part of the regular Stoic creed? Especially its pantheistic belief in the World-Soul, that is, in the divine origin of life and the share in the divine nature which every living thing can consequently claim. Further, the characteristically Stoic doctrine (though the Stoics were not the first to invent it) of the wickedness inherent in matter; and how evils of every kind spring from our material bodies — the excitements of passions and fears, of pain and pleasure. All this, you say, and say with truth, Vergil declares to us on the high authority of Anchises, and Anchises in Elysium. Why then look further for any philosophic attitude on Vergil's part, when his own utterances, in one of the latest parts of his work, seem to pledge him so clearly to a Stoic creed?

But to this question there is an answer. We must not judge Vergil's theory of life merely by one passage of twenty or thirty lines taken in isolation from the rest. I have no doubt that Vergil was wholly sincere in commending the Stoic doctrines just mentioned; and he certainly commended also the Stoic pursuit of virtue for its own sake. But if we ask whether he accepted their nominal ideal of philosophic calm, that is, of complete indifference to joy and to sorrow, as the aim of the philosopher's endeavour (that which we popularly understand by Stoicism today, and which was certainly part of their creed in Vergil's time and later), then, surely, truth compels us

---

[1] In both these scenes it is hardly fanciful to see reflections of Vergil's own experience — a recollection of the days when he trotted around the big farm of the Magii (see Chapter 2) beside his hard-working father; and a more tragic memory of the difficulty which he must have had in persuading his father, now an aged man, to fly from the farm when Antony's wild soldiery were breaking in. The story in Eclogue IX shows that they lingered till the last moment, and, like Anchises, were dislodged only by an omen.

to reply that in that sense Vergil was not a Stoic; nor was even Anchises, at the very height of his revelation, whatever he might preach. For Anchises rejoices keenly with Aeneas in the greatness of Rome to be;[1] and Anchises weeps over the bereavement which Rome suffered in the death of the young Marcellus.[2] When, therefore, Vergil puts upon the lips of Anchises[3] the famous Stoic doctrine that desire and fear, sorrow and joy, are all equally the fruit of our evil material condition, he does not and cannot mean, we may be sure, every kind of sorrow and every kind of joy, but only the selfish kinds, akin to the selfish fears and covetings which the first half of the maxim condemned. That is, clearly, the limit within which Vergil could accept or meant to accept the Stoic creed. Some joys and some sorrows were to Vergil the most precious part of life.

This brings us to my last and chief point — Vergil's attitude to what seemed to him the supreme paradox; the supreme example which proved the need of stating things by antithesis, of always seeing two sides to every human event. Let me state simply what I think to have been Vergil's view; and let me confess that my perception of what he felt has probably been quickened by the tragic experience of the European War of 1914–1918 — an experience only too closely resembling that of Vergil's generation in the eighteen years that preceded the battle of Actium. In studying the Golden Bough,[4] we saw that there was one thing which to Vergil was of paramount importance, and that was the affection of human beings — their affection, first, for their own human kind, secondly, for their fellow creatures, and thirdly, for the power which we call Nature, who to him was a Being not less throbbing with life and affection, not less bountiful of love to men, than any human mother to her child. Through the ages it is this which has endeared Vergil to thousands of unknown readers who, through the veil of mist raised by the strangeness of his tongue and the distance of his times from their own, have

[1] *Aen.*, VI, 718.   [2] VI, 868.
[3] VI, 733: *Hinc metuunt cupiuntque dolent gaudentque.*
[4] See p. 49, above.

felt the central, inner glow of his human affection, the pulse of that great heart. Think of his picture, in the *Georgics*,[1] of the farmer at home with his children 'hanging round his kisses'; recall the delight with which he notes the ways of animals small and great, but especially the small ones — birds and insects and little creatures of the soil; how more than once he makes an enthusiastic avowal of gratitude to the beneficent power that strews men's path with blessings. Remember that central line in the *Georgics*[2] where he is describing the bounty of Nature, even in the untilled forest and mountain, and breaks out with a cry of almost passionate feeling: 'And yet can men be slow to sow the ground and contribute their share of pains?'

But in the *Aeneid*, since it is less often read as a whole, perhaps we are less conscious of the frequency of the same note. With what sympathy does Vergil sketch the figure of every aged man, — Anchises, Evander, Latinus, — and of every youth — Pallas and Lausus, Nisus and Euryalus? When Galaesus is slain at the outbreak of the fighting in Book VII, failing in his effort to pacify his countrymen, have you noted how his flocks and herds at home and all the people of his farm are brought into the picture to represent the mourning for their master?[3] Think of the feeling shown for Silvia's pet stag, whose accidental wounding by Ascanius, in his hunt, is the signal for the outbreak of war. This incident is actually censured by a learned and thoughtful modern critic as merely pretty (*genrehaft*) and Alexandrine, quite beneath the dignity of the epic.

Above all, remember those to whom Vergil gives the highest honour in Elysium, the snow-white crown:[4] warriors who have suffered wounds in defence of their country (*ob patriam*, not *pro patria* merely[5]); high-minded priests and poets, worthy of

---

[1] II, 523.
[2] II, 433: *et dubitant homines serere atque impendere curam?* The line is certainly Vergilian and appropriate to the passage as a whole (429–454, with 516–522), whether or not it now stands exactly in the place that Vergil intended—a question which our manuscript evidence leaves, perhaps, in doubt.
[3] VII, 538; and in XII, 517, the fate of Menoetes is told with a like touch.
[4] VI, 660–665.
[5] The difference (*e. g.*, from Horace, *Odes*, III, 2. 13) is worth noting.

their calling; those who have found new arts and made life
more fair; and, last of all, 'those who by good deeds have
made two or three folk remember them' —

quique sui memores aliquos fecere merendo.

This line Eduard Norden has strangely misrepresented in his
eloquent translation by inserting the word *Herrscher* ('rulers
of men') as antecedent to the relative *qui*. Norden had in
mind a passage of Pindar, which, no doubt, Vergil knew; but
see the difference Vergil made. Rulers of men! Why, what
Vergil promised, though it is a glory which an emperor might
covet, is one that a slave could win.

But I need not prolong this enumeration. Let me ask you,
finally, to realise the tragic contradiction which Vergil found
beneath this lovingkindness of the world — the fact that our
human affection is the source both of the only joys worth
counting joys and of the only sorrows worth counting sorrows.
Every one of the troubles of the *Aeneid*, every one of its tragedies, springs ultimately from this: the tragedy of Dido, first
from the misguided affections of Juno and Venus, and then
from her own; the tragedy of Juturna, from her love for her
brother; the war in Latium, from Silvia's affection for her stag
and her followers' affection for Silvia. And the second war,
from Turnus' love for Lavinia and his followers' devotion to
Turnus; the tragedies of Brutus and Torquatus, briefly mentioned in the vision of Anchises; and the tragedy of Marcellus,
at the end — the essence of all these lies in the affection of
some men or women, ill guided or ill governed, or crossed by
physical calamity. Has it ever been realised that, with the sol-
itary exception of Drances (who plays but a small part), there
is no such motive in the whole of the *Aeneid* as that from which
the *Iliad* starts — the high-handed selfishness of one primitive
chieftain compensating himself by robbing another? Compare and contrast with this [1] the crowning scene of the *Aeneid*,
in which the conquered Turnus might have been spared but for
what, to the ancient mind, was his inhuman cruelty to Pallas

---

[1] And still more with Homer's picture (in *Iliad*, XXII) of Achilles rejecting Hector's prayer for burial and wishing he could tear his victim to pieces with his teeth.
C'est magnifique mais — it is in a different universe. See also p. 65, above.

and his father, of which he still wore the trophy in the baldric of Pallas girt upon his own shoulder. Such an offender could not survive into the new era; the violence of Turnus would continue to trample on the laws of humanity. But even Turnus, Vergil could not doom without a note of pity, for his violence sprang from his love. In the last words of the whole epic the soul of Turnus passes 'indignant to the shades.'

So it was in this common source of human sorrow and human joy that Vergil found the ultimate enigma which for him wrapped the world in mystery. Strange as the contradiction was, he held it to be the key of life.

Here, then, we have reached the centre of Vergil's thought. All the sorrow and all the joy of the universe seemed to him to spring from one root, and he accepts — nay, he welcomes — them both. There could be no human affection, so Vergil saw, unless it were such as to make its possessors capable, and capable in equal degrees, both of the most exquisite suffering and of the most exquisite joy. This to him is the fundamental fact of the universe — that all pain and all joy are to be measured simply in terms of human love. And if you ask him his last word upon this mystery, a mystery on which he has pondered year after year, viewing it from both sides, through all his study of life, he will tell you that the Golden Bough is always found in the shadows of the forest, when it is sought in fulfilment of duty. And while others may turn away from the sight or thought of those shadows in mere dread or disbelief, Vergil will bid us, like his hero, pluck the bough eagerly and trust it gratefully, to bring us through even darker shadows out into the light beyond; to trust that somewhere, somehow, Death itself is overcome by the power and persistence of Love.

VIII

THE PORTRAIT OF A ROMAN NOBLE[1]

SOME years ago, the study of the text of Livy's First Decade suggested to me a lecture [2] the object of which was to point out his kinship of spirit with the great Italian painters like Titian and Giorgione, who sprang from his own Venetic stock. This kinship is especially clear in the warmth of his imagination and in his lively sympathy with the persons who appear in his story. The leading characters of the early Books, in a series of famous stories, give us an embodiment of some of the most typical Roman virtues, set, as Livy writes in his preface, each 'in some shining example.' For many of these stories in the form in which they were current in Livy's day — for example, that of Coriolanus — the historical evidence then available was in many ways unworthy of trust. But the central situation and the behaviour of the chief characters, as, for example, the yielding of Coriolanus to his mother's entreaties, are in every instance so typically Roman that, even if all the names and all the dates were false, which is by no means the case, the stories themselves would still be ideally true. They represent what the Romans believed, and liked to believe, of their own past. That belief was a part of their history, and a part of great importance in the creative age in which Livy began to write and with which the present volume is concerned.[3]

But when we pass to Livy's Third Decade, which records the great Punic War, from 219 to 201 B.C., we are well within the historical period. What difficulties there are now in our study arise not from the dearth but from the multitude of authorities; and in many details Livy, as he frankly points out, has

---

[1] This chapter is based upon a lecture first delivered in the John Rylands Library in September, 1922.

[2] See *Great Inheritance*, chap. 9, on "The Venetian Point of View in Roman History."

[3] This point was nobly illustrated by the late Dr. Warde Fowler, in *Roman Studies and Interpretations*, p. 8.

not reached certainty in his efforts to disentangle conflicting accounts and to analyse what we may call the authorised version of events. But he was always and everywhere keenly interested in men and women; and I believe it is true to say that he spared no pains at all in forming and expressing with delicate precision a judgement on all the conspicuous persons in Roman history. We can, of course, speak only of the periods on which his work has survived; that we do not possess his studies of Caesar, Pompey, and the Gracchi is one of the calamities of literature. But in following the main lines of the story of the third century B.C. we are on firm ground; and without anxiety about the substance, we are free to study the imagination with which Livy has made his characters live and move.

The insight with which he handled this part of his work we may estimate by studying his delineation of a single personality. Take the figure which, in fact, occupies far the largest space given to any character in the thirty-five Books which have survived, appearing in no less than fourteen of them, and being the central topic through at least one, the twenty-eighth. I mean the personality of Publius Cornelius Scipio Africanus, the only Roman general who was a match for Hannibal, and the man who brought the whole eighteen years of war to an end by conquering Spain, invading Africa, and at last defeating Hannibal at Zama in 202 B.C. It is a figure quite central in the history of the Roman Republic, and of this Livy was fully conscious. Scipio's strength and Scipio's weaknesses, such as they were, embodied the strength and the weaknesses of the Republic itself. In them culminated its triumph; in them lay the seeds of its decay. Such, at least, is Livy's plain verdict; but it is a verdict which, I venture to say, might have been hard for us to reach without his critical study. From the Greek historian, Polybius, whose life long touched that of the Scipionic circle, and whom, so far as he went, Livy carefully and frankly followed, we should derive a conception of Scipio's character, which, though it is nowhere inconsistent with Livy's picture, is yet in details so far less critical as to be incomplete and almost unconvincing; a conception so uniformly superhuman, so wanting in light and shade, as to leave us to wonder why such a man ever had any enemies.

Let us review some of the more striking scenes in Scipio's life. As we proceed, we shall note certain points of difference between the record of Livy and that of Polybius.

Recall first the situation when Scipio received his first commission, in 211 B.C. His father and his father's brother had both been defeated and killed in Spain; the Romans had been driven north of the Ebro, and their whole authority in the country endangered. In Italy, after his great victories at Trebia, Trasimene, and Cannae, Hannibal had moved almost where he would;[1] and in the previous year he had pitched his camp three miles from the walls of Rome and had ridden up to the Colline Gate, though he did not venture even then to attack the city itself, and had failed to relieve Capua.

But Spain was the real key to the struggle. In Spain Hannibal had trained his army, and from Spain he expected reinforcement. The Senate for once shrank from the responsibility of appointing a commander, and set a dangerous precedent by referring the appointment to the popular assembly. The popular vote unanimously chose Scipio, though he was a young man of twenty-four. He had held no military office whatever, though he had served in one campaign with his father.

Consider first the account of one side of his character which Polybius[2] gives; I quote from Shuckburgh's excellent version:

Now it seems to me that in his character and views Publius was very like Lycurgus. For we must not suppose that it was from superstition that Lycurgus continually consulted the Pythian priestess in establishing the Lacedaemonian constitution; nor that Scipio depended on dreams and ominous words for his success. But as both saw that the majority of mankind cannot be got to accept contentedly what is new and strange, or to face dangers with courage, without some hope of divine favour — Lycurgus, by always supporting his own schemes with an oracular response from the Pythia, secured better acceptation for his ideas; and Scipio, by always instilling into the minds of the vulgar an opinion of his acting on some divine suggestion, caused those under his command to confront danger with greater courage. But that he invariably

---

[1] This period is described in Chapter 6, above.
[2] Polybius, X, 2, 3, 4, and 5.

acted on calculation and with foresight, and that the successful issue of his plans was always in harmony with rational expectation, will be evident.

One typical example of this we may note in passing. By a study of the tides Scipio had ascertained that on a given day and hour a lagoon by which New Carthage was on one side defended would be merely shallow water. Hence by an assault made through this lagoon he was able to take the city by a surprise. But he had led his army to believe that Neptune was giving them miraculous assistance.[1] Now hear Polybius again:

That Scipio was beneficent and high-minded is acknowledged; but that he was acute, sober-minded, and earnest in pursuit of his aims, no one will admit, except those who have lived with him and contemplated his character, so to speak, in broad daylight. Of such Gaius Laelius was one. He took part in everything Scipio did or said from boyhood to the day of his death; and it was he who convinced me of this. . . .

Once, when his elder brother Lucius was a candidate for the Aedileship, his mother was going round to the temples and sacrificing on behalf of that brother. His father was then on his voyage to Spain. Publius Scipio therefore said to his mother that he had had a dream and seen the same vision twice: namely, that he was coming home from the Forum after being elected Aedile with his brother, and that she met them at the door and threw her arms round them and kissed them. His mother with womanly feeling exclaimed, "Oh that I might see that day!" He replied, "Would you like us to try?" Upon her assenting, under the idea that he would not venture, but was only jesting on the spur of the moment (for of course he was quite a young man), he begged her to prepare him[2] at once a white toga, such as it is the custom for candidates for office to wear.

His mother did so, and thought no more about it: but Publius, having obtained the white toga, went to the Forum before his mother was awake [and was elected Aedile]. . . . The news having been suddenly brought to their mother, she rushed in the utmost delight to meet and salute them at the door. Accordingly Publius was believed by all who had heard previously about his dream to have held commune with the gods. But in point of fact there was

---

[1] Livy, XXVI, 45. 9.

[2] From this it may be gathered that a Roman noble was even more dependent upon his womankind for a correct attire than any householder of today.

no dream at all.   Scipio was kind, open-handed, and courteous, and by these means had conciliated the favour of the multitude.   But by a dexterous use of the occasion, both with the people and with his mother, he obtained his purpose, and moreover got the reputation of acting under divine inspiration.

Modern students of psychology, who have learnt that our dreams are often connected with our desires, may not think it necessary to assume as calmly as Polybius does, that Scipio merely invented the whole story.

Now there is little in this sketch which Livy does not confirm, but there are some sides or aspects of the character on which Polybius is quite silent that are brought out by Livy's more critical and sympathetic insight — an insight no doubt sharpened by a knowledge of the political history of Rome after Polybius' time.

Hear now Livy's much shorter characterisation, and note the questions which he raises, but leaves open for his readers to judge:

[Scipio was undoubtedly the possessor of striking gifts; but besides this he had from childhood studied the art of their effective display.   Whether there was some vein of superstition in his own temperament, or whether it was with the aim of securing for his commands the authority of inspired utterances, he rarely spoke in public without pretending to some nocturnal vision or supernatural suggestion.   In order to impress public opinion in this direction, he had made a practice, from the day he reached manhood, of never engaging in any business, public or private, without first paying a visit to the Capitol.   There he would enter the sanctuary and pass some time, generally in solitude and seclusion.   This habit, from which he never deviated, made converts in some circles to a belief, to which accident or design had given wide currency, that his origin was other than human.] There was a story once widely believed about Alexander the Great, that his male parent had been a huge serpent, often seen in his mother's chamber but vanishing directly men appeared.   This miracle was told again of Scipio with the same picturesque absurdity, but he himself never cast ridicule upon it; indeed, he rather lent it countenance by the course which he adopted of neither wholly disclaiming such tales nor openly asserting their truth.

Now observe that in this account, brief as it is, Livy gives room for the possibility of some sincere piety on Scipio's part;

and it seems indeed doubtful whether his habit of daily visits to the Capitol could have been maintained for so long without it. And this is strongly confirmed by his action in the Syrian War in 190 B.C.,— an action by which he had nothing to gain, and by which he and his brother had very much to lose, — in keeping the army waiting at the Hellespont for many days, until the last day of March, because he was a Salian Priest and bound by rule to stop where he was until the month was ended.[1]

We see then that, on the one hand, Livy allows for some degree of religious belief in Scipio's mind; but that, on the other hand, he cannot take the entirely cheerful view that Polybius does of the element of fraud in Scipio's use of religion. Neither can he conceal a characteristic in Scipio which it is difficult to name, but which we may perhaps call his super-self-confidence, his extraordinary personal exaltation. Following Livy, Aulus Gellius expresses it in a happy phrase — *conscientia sui subnixus* ('lifted high on his consciousness of himself'). Let us take only two examples, the first from a speech[2] in the Senate in 205 B.C. Here is the conclusion of his answer to Fabius Cunctator, who had spoken at length, making much of his own part in the war, and little of Scipio's. The rendering (with those that follow) is mainly Philemon Holland's.

'It shall content and suffice me to have thus far spoken about the public interest and the war presently in hand; and concerning the provinces now in question. But it would require a long and tedious discourse, and the same irrelevant altogether unto you, if, as Q. Fabius hath set himself to make light of my work in Spain, so I likewise should diminish and make a mock of his glory, but set out myself and mine own reputation with magnificent words. My lords of the Senate, I will do neither the one nor the other. And if in nothing else, yet at least, young man as I am, in modesty and government of my tongue, I will go beyond him, old as he is. Thus have I lived and thus have I carried myself in mine actions, that without speech I can easily content myself with that opinion which you of yourselves may have conceived and entertain of me.'

Scipio is too modest to praise himself; yet he pats himself on the back for being more modest than Fabius, and suggests

---

[1] Livy, XXXVII, 33. 7.   [2] XXVIII, 44. 16.

gently that, after all, to praise what he, Scipio, had done, would be quite superfluous!

The second example is from his answer to the envoys of King Antiochus in the Syrian War in 190 B.C. Antiochus had sent them with a great sum of money and the offer to liberate Scipio's son whom he had captured, if he, Scipio, would influence the Roman general to make a favourable peace.[1] This is the speech, according to Livy:[2]

'That you neither know the Romans all in general, nor myself in particular unto whom you were sent, I less marvel, when I see that you are altogether ignorant of the state of the fortunes of him who hath sent you hither . . . for whom nothing now remains but to submit to whatever we ordain. For myself, as concerning my son, I will accept it as a great present, beseeming the munificence of a king, should he send him to me again; but of his other present, while I pray Heaven that my estate may never have need of such gifts, my mind for certain never will. And for the great offer the king maketh unto me, of my son, he shall find me thankful unto him, if it please him (for this private benefit unto me done) to require at my hands a private favour again; but as touching the public weal, he shall pardon me, that I will neither receive ought from him, nor bestow any thing upon him. And all I can bestow on him at this present is to give him good and faithful counsel. Go your ways, and tell him from me, to abstain from war, and not to refuse any condition of peace whatsoever.'

Of this exaltation the traces are comparatively few in Polybius' picture, though it was undoubtedly this more than anything else that roused the bitter animosity from which Scipio suffered in his later years. On the other hand, Livy's picture of the man is in some ways much more attractive. He allows room, first, as we have seen, for some actual piety in Scipio's own mind, which redeems him from the merely brutal insincerity which Polybius assumes. But, secondly, Livy recognises the delicate insight with which Scipio penetrates to the real feelings of the people with whom he dealt, a gift which was the secret of his extraordinary diplomatic success. This appears plainly in his speeches and acts.

[1] The account in Polybius (XXI, 12) is much the same, but quite without the personal touch; in Polybius' account Scipio lays no stress on the difference between private and public action.
[2] Livy, XXVII, 36.

I would commend it in passing as an interesting literary and historical exercise (for, say, any Classical Sixth Form) to note the differences between the parallel versions of the speeches given by Polybius and Livy respectively. Two of the speeches are especially characteristic — that to the mutineers at Sucro, and that to Hannibal in the interview before the battle of Zama.

The mutiny at Sucro in 206 B.C. was one of the most dangerous points in Scipio's career, as it threatened the Roman supremacy in Spain at a moment when it seemed finally assured. Scipio had been ill, the Roman government had been dilatory with the soldiers' pay, and the soldiers had actually chosen certain obscure persons rejoicing in the names of Atrius and Albius to replace their generals. Scipio handled the dangerous situation in a masterly way, securing all the ringleaders beforehand, and deluding the mutineers into thinking that all his loyal troops had been dispatched far away from the town. Of the speech which he made to them when they, mainly unarmed, and without their leaders, surrounded his tribunal and were themselves surrounded by loyal troops, Polybius and Livy give reports which in substance are identical, but in style so different that they could hardly be thought the utterance of the same man. I greatly doubt whether any mutineer who heard the speech which Polybius gives would have been influenced by any motive but that of fear; whereas Livy makes him appeal to the warmest personal feelings of the soldiers, their old loyalty to Rome, their sympathy for their general newly recovered from illness, and their gratitude for the forgiveness which he promises. In Livy's story, Scipio seems to enter into the feelings of the mutineers with a quite divine comprehension. He even arouses their sense of humour against themselves, — a sentiment which teachers know to be a powerful element in penitence, — by dwelling on the ill-omened names of their chosen leaders, Atrius and Albius, "Blackie" and "Whitie," a thing which Scipio, like every Roman, was very likely to do, with a certain degree of real belief in the omen. The crowning touch is where he puts on a level in the same sentence his own sickness of body with their sickness of mind, followed by an impassioned expression of his grief at their unfaithfulness.

One small but significant indication of the difference in the colour of the two accounts deserves special mention, and it admits of demonstration. The speech in Polybius contains some 520 words, in which pronouns or verbal forms of the first person singular occur 14 times — that is, once in every 37 words. In Livy the speech occupies about 1025 words, and there are no less than 64 occurrences of *ego*, or *meus*, or verbs in the first person singular — that is, one word in every 16; a frequency more than double.

I wish it were possible here to study the speeches in full; but perhaps the last paragraph will be enough to give some picture of Scipio's attitude.

Here is the end of the speech given [1] by Polybius:

'I should like then to ask — what was it in which you trusted? Surely not in the skill and valour of the leaders whom you have now elected, or in the fasces and axes which were borne in front of them — men of whom I will not deign to say even another word. All this, soldiers, is absolutely futile; nor will you be able to allege even the smallest just complaint against me or your country. Wherefore I will undertake your defence to Rome and myself, by putting forward a plea that all the world will acknowledge to hold good. And it is, that a crowd is ever easily misled and easily induced to any error. Therefore it is that crowds are like the sea, which in its own nature is safe and quiet; but when the winds fall violently upon it, assumes the character of the blasts which lash it into fury; thus a multitude also is ever found to be what its leaders and counsellors are. Acting on this consideration, I and my fellow-officers hereby offer you pardon and amnesty for the past; but to the guilty authors of the mutiny we are resolved to show no mercy, but to punish them as their misconduct to their country and to ourselves deserves.'

Here is Livy's version [2] of the same:

'But what grief of heart, what fit of anger hath incited and provoked you? Grant that your wages were paid later by a few days, whilst your General lay sick; was that a sufficient cause for you to proclaim open war against your country? Was that enough to cause you to revolt from the people of Rome, and turn to the Iler-

---

[1] XI, 29.   [2] XXVIII, 29. 2-8.

getes, and to spare no law of God and man, and make shipwreck of conscience and common honesty? Surely, soldiers, you were distraught and out of your wits. I was not myself prostrated by a more powerful sickness in my body, than ye were in your mind and understanding. I tremble to think or say what folk believed, what they hoped, what they wished. Let all be forgotten, if it be possible; if not, let us not speak of it, howsoever we do, but cover it up in silence. I cannot deny that my words have seemed harsh and bitter unto you; but how much more cruel think ye, are your deeds? And if ye deem it reasonable that I should bear the things that ye have done, can ye not abide even to hear them all recounted? But even these matters shall be no more laid against you from henceforth. Would God ye could as soon forget them, as I will. And therefore as touching you all in general, if ye repent for your folly, I shall be content, and think you punished to the full. But as for Albius Calenus and Atrius Umber, with the rest of the authors of this detestable mutiny, they shall make amends for their transgression, with their life's blood. The spectacle of their punishment ought not to seem unto you grievous, but rather a pleasant and delectable sight, if ye be come again to your right mind. For their intent did no more cruel hurt and mischief to any man than to yourselves.'

Of the speech to Hannibal, the two records are even closer, so that the variations can be pointed out with precision; and yet between them there is a world of difference. The whole way through, in Polybius' account, Scipio reasons with Hannibal as with an equal. In Livy, he talks to him as Jehovah might have done to the defeated Satan in *Paradise Lost*. Take two sentences as typical of the difference. In referring to Hannibal's reluctant departure from Italy, according to Polybius, Scipio said only, 'You left Italy unwillingly.' But in Livy he said (to use Holland's version, which is not at all too vigorous), 'I have haled and drawn you into Africa by strong arm, all the shuffling and resistance you could make to the contrary notwithstanding' (*prope manu conserta restitantem ac tergiuersantem in Africam attraxerim*). And while, at the end, Polybius briefly states one of the alternatives before Hannibal in the words, 'or you must conquer us in a battle' (ἢ μαχομένους νικᾶν), the speech in Livy ends with seven words, every one of which has a sting: *bellum parate quoniam pacem pati non potuistis.*

eturned thither with Masi-
.ad now to deal with the delicate
lis bride. The captive Syphax, who
st and friend, now warned him that
who had perverted him, her first husband, from
his former loyalty to Rome, would be sure to pervert Masinissa
in his turn.

It is impossible, as we read the story, not to feel that in writing it Livy was thinking deeply of certain great events of his own times.

Scipio had once refused the title of king on the ground that the title of Imperator given him by his soldiers was a nobler thing; and in this Livy was certainly thinking of the craving for the shows of Oriental kingship which had been fatal to Julius Caesar, and of the care with which Augustus had put such things behind him. And so, when Livy records how Masinissa was persuaded by Scipio's grave but gentle appeal to put away the beautiful Carthaginian woman who had captivated him on the day on which he took her captive, we may be certain that the historian was thinking both of Vergil's picture of Dido and of the great historical parallel which dominated Vergil's thought, the story of Cleopatra, the ruin which she brought on Antony, the stern refusal of Augustus even to set eyes upon his captive, and her suicide which followed that refusal.

Now hear Livy's account:[1]

Therefore Scipio was driven into no small anxiety, and wist not well what to make of it. The marriage had been so huddled up, as it were, in the midst of the operations of war, without the advice of Laelius, without even awaiting his arrival. Such headlong haste had Masinissa made without any advisement, that the very same day that he first set eye upon the enemy queen his prisoner, he must needs espouse and marry her out of hand, in the very house of his greatest enemy. Moreover, these matters seemed the more shameful, in that Scipio himself, during the time that he had been in Spain, young as he was, had been never enamoured upon the beauty of any captive woman. As he revolved these things in his mind,

[1] XXX, 14. 15 ff.

Laelius and Masinissa arrived in
comed them both alike, and showed th
yea and honoured them with singular pr
openly in a full audience of his staff, he to
spoke unto him thus. "I suppose, Masinissa, that you
some good parts, for love whereof, both at the first yo
duced to come into Spain and contract amity with me; and afterwards also in Africa, you reposed yourself and all your hopes in my
fidelity and protection. But of all those virtues, for which I have
seemed worthy of your affection, there is not one wherein I have so
much gloried, as in the temperance and bridling of carnal pleasures.
This virtue, Masinissa, I could wish that you also would have
joined unto the rest that are in you so rare and excellent. For our
age (trust me truly) stands not so much in danger of armed enemies,
as of those temptations to pleasure that compass us on every side.
And he that by his sober governance hath been able to rule and
tame the same, hath won more honour, and gotten a greater victory than we have done by the subduing of Syphax. What valiant
exploits and worthy deeds you have achieved in mine absence,
I have willingly published, and still remember. But for the rest,
I would rather you would consider of them by yourself, than blush
if I rehearsed them to you. Through the good fortune, and by the
forces of the people of Rome, Syphax is vanquished and taken
prisoner. And therefore, himself, his wife, his realm, his lands,
his towns, the inhabitants, and in fine whatsoever belonged unto
Syphax, are become the booty of the people of Rome. The king
himself and the queen his wife, even had she not been born a citizen
of Carthage, even had we not seen her father to be the grand cap-
tain of our enemies, ought by right to have been sent to Rome, that
the Senate and people of Rome might pass their censure and judgement upon her, who is reported to have alienated a confederate king
from us and to have caused him rashly to take arms against us.
Strive then to master your affections; take heed you stain not many
good virtues with one fault. Mar not the grace of so many worthy
deserts, by one trespass which is far more considerable in itself than
is the person that has been the occasion thereof." . . .

As he heard this, Masinissa not merely blushed deeply, but broke
into tears; and promising that he would submit to the General's
commands but entreating him as far as might be to have regard to
the pledge he, Masinissa, had rashly given, he retired to his tent
altogether overcome.

There all by himself, after he had passed some time in many sighs
and sobs, as could easily be overheard by them that stood about the
tent, at the last he gave one grievous groan above the rest, and
called for one of his trusty grooms, who had under his hand (as the

manner was of princes) the keeping of a special poison, against all doubtful chances that might happen. This poison he commanded him to mix in a goblet of wine, and to carry it to Sophonisba, and withall to tell her thus much from him. That Masinissa would have been most willing to perform the plighted troth and first promise, which an husband ought unto his wedded wife. But since superior powers, and those that were mightier than himself, had bereft him of that liberty, he was ready and able yet to accomplish his second pledge, namely, that she should not come alive into the hands of the Romans; and therefore he advised her, that remembering that noble commander her father and her native country and the two kings to whom she had been married, she would provide for herself and save her own honour. This message, together with the poison, the servant, when he was come unto Sophonisba delivered unto her. Whereat quoth she, "I accept this marriage present, and welcome it is unto me, if this be the best token that my husband could find to send unto his wife. Yet thus much tell him again from me, that I would have been better content to die, if my marriage-bed had not stood so near to my grave [*si non in fumere meo nupsissem*]." She spake not more proudly than she acted, for she took the cup in hand, and showing no sign at all of fear, she roundly drank it off. When the tidings came to Scipio, for fear lest the proud and passionate young prince might do himself some mischief in his sorrow, he sent for him forthwith; and gave him now good and comfortable words, and now gently rebuked, in that he had thought to make amends for one act of folly with another, and to bring it all to a more cruel and tragical conclusion than need had been. The next day to the end that he might withdraw his mind away from this present turmoil of self-reproach, Scipio mounted up into his tribunal, and bade them call the army to an audience. There first, he openly styled Masinissa by the name of King, and honoured him with rare commendations; which done, he gave him a golden crown, a golden cup, a chair of state and a sceptre, both of ivory, a rich Roman robe embroidered in divers colours with palms of victory. To these gifts he added words of honour. For, said he, as there is nothing among the Romans more stately and magnificent than a triumph, so they that ride in triumph, have no ornament more glorious than these of which the people of Rome esteemeth, among all strangers and aliens, none to be worthy save Masinissa alone.

By these honours the king's hard thoughts were no little softened, and the hope kindled in him to be made sovereign of all Numidia.

If I had the whole of this lecture, instead of its last sentence, still before me, I could not hope to do justice, in any explicit comment, to the tragical pity and, withal, the Roman majesty of Livy's story, nor to the subtle and vivid picture which it gives of the characters of Sophonisba, of Masinissa, and of Scipio himself. I must be content to commend it to your private study and delight, as a crowning example of Livy's critical and imaginative power.

THE ARCHITECTURE OF THE EPIC [1]

THE title of this lecture may, I fear, suggest a rather ponderous treatment of a ponderous subject. When I began to put together what I chiefly wanted to say and to read what others had said, I confess that I was reminded, by contrast, of a remark made once by an American friend of mine who had been studying the commentary of an Anglican divine on the Minor Prophets. "I do not know when I learnt such a heap of things," he said, shaking his head sadly, "such a heap of things that were not so." My trouble was the opposite — I seemed to be smothered by a heap of things that were so and always would be; and the definite matters which I wanted to discuss seemed likely to be drowned in a flood of respectable doctrines which demanded a passing homage. The only way to escape is to be brief and dogmatic in stating one or two general principles, and then to apply them to the structure of the *Aeneid*, about which there are, I venture to think, some questions on which light may still be sought.

After all, although the materials of architecture are heavy enough, its greatest triumphs are distinguished by the impression which they give of lightness, allied with organic strength, when a whole building seems to be not dead stone but a living growth, almost moveable and flexible, playing with the sunlight, not blotting it out, communing with the breezes of Heaven as with friends, not enemies.

One such building I have in mind is the new Marischal College of Aberdeen, built, I suppose, of the heaviest and hardest stone in the world; yet so exquisitely planned that on a sunny day it has all the delicate charm of filigree silver. Another, if an Englishman may dare to say so, is the *Tribune* tower in

---

[1] This lecture was first delivered in the John Rylands Library in January, 1925; it is here printed in the revised form in which it was given at Harvard in May, 1927. As usual, I am profoundly indebted, especially in the verse renderings, to the wise and generous criticism of my friend Professor W. B. Anderson, Litt.D.

Chicago. And but for the sooty conditions under which the ignorance or greed of some individuals in Manchester condemn its citizens to draw their breath, something like this would be felt, every day, of the lovely building of the John Rylands Library. Every great poem gives us a similar sense of living, organic unity. How is it attained in the epic?

Few epics have stood the test of time: the *Iliad* and *Odyssey*, the *Aeneid*, the *Divina Commedia* of Dante, and Milton's *Paradise Lost*. Of course, there are others; but none (in Europe, at all events) which are not in close relation with the Vergilian and Homeric models. The best description of an epic known to me is given in that brilliant book, *English Lessons for English People*, the joint work of the historian, J. R. Seeley, and the great scholar and teacher, Dr. Edwin Abbott. They laid down that an epic poem is a chapter in the history of Providence; that is to say, it must show the working out of some providential purpose in a given period of history.

In a less theological shape, the definition means that an epic must be felt as a single narrative leading straight to some result of at least national magnitude — possibly more than national, but at least national. The sorrows and the courage of Enoch Arden or Miles Standish, or the anxieties of Bishop Blougram, may interest us keenly, but their experiences are not of epic magnitude. Some one may quote Mr. Kipling's prudent maxim:

> There are six-and-sixty ways of constructing tribal lays,
> And every single one of them is right.

That may be so; and yet, for one lecture, one of the sixty-six may suffice.

Starting thus, we discover quickly that there are two or three practical consequences in the structure of an epic which have been, in fact, observed by poets. Obvious enough you may think them; but they have contributed a good deal to the shaping of the *Aeneid*.

1. *Never end at the end*. History never stops, and if any set of events has a real historical importance, that importance will not be ended by the point at which its character is first determined. The story of the *Iliad* is epic partly because it looks

forward to the triumph of the Greeks and back to the guilt of Troy. The purport of Dante's vision was not ended when he resumed his life as a mortal man in Italy after his marvellous journey; who can regard the whole *Commedia* as merely a nine-days incident of the poet's private life, although that is what he represented it to be? We may well be shy of devising a formula for the scope of Dante's undertaking; but it certainly was something which pictured the contribution of Italy, past, present, and future, to the intellectual and spiritual growth of Europe; and that, happily, as we know and as Dante knew, was not to end with Easter week in 1300.

On the other hand, a poem must end somewhere; there should be some concrete incident at the end, in which the reader feels that the picture has found its frame. Of this need our own Milton was conscious. The substantial end of *Paradise Lost* is the final victory of the Redeemer prophesied by Michael:

> New Heav'ns, new earth, ages of endless date
> Founded in righteousness, and peace, and love.

This is line 551 of the last Book of *Paradise Lost;* but what happens in the 88 lines that remain? Adam and Eve are expelled from Paradise by Michael and the cherubim.

> The world was all before them, where to choose
> Their place of rest, and Providence their guide.
> They, hand in hand with wand'ring steps and slow,
> Through Eden took their solitary way.

These beautiful lines mark the end of the poem, but not the goal of its story.

2. The second principle is even more obvious: *Never begin at the beginning.* The pictures of past history, personal and more than personal, national and more than national, which make up so much of the *Divina Commedia*, range over all the centuries; and the date with which Dante happens to connect the beginning of his vision, the eve of Good Friday, A.D. 1300, has only this importance — it separates his visions of the past from his vision of the future.[1] In *Paradise Lost* what is really

---

[1] Of course, many of the incidents foretold in the *Commedia* had happened before the poem was written, although the date which Dante had chosen, partly for this

the earliest event, the revolt of Satan, is related by Raphael in
Books V and VI; and the next step in Miltonic history, the
creation of this world, is not begun until Book VII, or com-
pleted until Book VIII, although we knew it had happened as
early as Book I, when Satan submits the rumour of it to his
infernal council. This council leads to Satan's journey to explore the new world for himself, which takes up the whole of
Books II and III.

The origin of this fashion was more or less accidental. In the
world to which the Homeric lays were first recited, the professional bard who recited them held a place of honour. Therefore, of course, in the world of yesterday, only yesterday, of
which the bard made a picture, there must be room for his own
high calling; consequently, while the story deals with the deeds
of yesterday, there will be parts of it in which a bard is represented as telling stories of the day before. In the *Iliad* we all
know how particular lays serve a retrospective purpose: for
example, the narratives in which the warriors glorify their
lineage before they engage in single combat, especially the
famous case of Glaucon and Diomede in Book VI. And the
delightful genius[1] which determined the present form of the
Odyssey set the adventures which Odysseus relates to his host,
Alcinous, in the four Books, IX–XII. These Books carry the
narrative from the fall of Troy down to Odysseus' arrival at the
island of Calypso, his fortunes after leaving Calypso having
been told more briefly by him in Book VII.

But why has such a convention maintained itself? "One
good custom" does not hold the world for centuries merely
because it is old. What are its advantages? They may be
summed up by saying that this practice of retrospective narrative makes the poem more like actual experience; because, as
we all know, we have to make the acquaintance of new people
every day, and we judge them very largely from the things

very purpose, made it necessary to depict them under the guise of prophecy. This
ex post facto prophecy must be distinguished from a poet's real anticipation of what,
at the time of his writing, is still to come.

[1] Whether the genius of one man or of a school of men, we must not stay to discuss; like most English scholars, I find it hard to disbelieve in some one controlling
intellect at this stage.

they first happen to say in our hearing; but their previous history we learn only afterwards, if at all. In this point the epic method is closely akin to that of the drama; the poet can shape the style of the narrator. It is generally his own story which he tells; and to represent a man talking about his own experience is to depict his character without seeming to do so.

3. The third principle is this: *The story must be varied, but not broken*. The episodes must not be digressions; they must all contribute to the central current; that is what Apollonius Rhodius and the other Alexandrines failed to understand. So they could not write epics: they wrote moderately entertaining narratives, of which Ovid's *Metamorphosis* [1] is the cleverest example.

Now, the most effective disturbance to any train of ideas is laughter. Unluckily not all disturbances produce laughter, but for laughter one's ideas or conduct must be interrupted; no interruption, no laughter. You must be surprised; *ridiculum secat res*, as Horace knew, cuts sharply, not merely slackens or softens, much less forwards or helps the immediate prospect; though, by breaking that to pieces, it may clear the air.

But where does this come into the epic? It does not come in, and must not. This is what we mean by epic dignity. Hence we reach a fourth maxim: *Smile, but never laugh aloud*. One passage in the *Iliad* and one in the *Odyssey* in which the architect of each has admitted farcical matter of a rather barbarous type, — if Professor Gilbert Murray's expurgatory theory be right, — the cozening of Jove and the trapping of Mars by Vulcan, have been condemned as un-epic by all critics, in ancient times and in our own day.

Turn now to the *Aeneid*. In the single Books of that poem nothing, I believe, reveals to us so intimately Vergil's governing thought as the way in which he has arranged his matter. In a former lecture [2] I have traced the gradual ascent of the idea of the Sixth Book, through the Approach and the Journey, to

---

[1] I welcome Professor D. A. Slater's interesting evidence showing that Ovid's title was in the singular (see his *Towards a Text of Ovid's Metamorphosis*, Oxford, 1927).

[2] *Great Inheritance*, chap. 6.

the Revelation, culminating in the Vision of Anchises. In the Second Book, who can forget the succession of the three great Acts of the tragedy? The first is in the sunlight and freedom of the fields outside the city of Troy, enjoyed by the Trojans for the first time for ten years; the army with the king himself, and indeed the whole people, swarming over the shore and exulting in their apparent deliverance from their Greek invaders, of whom the only trace left is the gaunt wooden horse alone on the plain. In the midst of this immense rejoicing, strange things happen — the capture of Sinon followed by his crafty story, and then the protest of Laocoön and his subsequent destruction by the serpents, ending in the triumphant return of the multitude to Troy with the wooden horse in their midst. The second Act leads to the climax of the tragedy in a series of closely related scenes, in all of which Aeneas takes part: first, his vision of Hector; then, the shifting phases of the fighting in the streets, followed by his attempt from the roof of the palace to repulse the assault of the Greeks on its walls, ended by the inrush of Pyrrhus and his slaughter of Priam. All this is at night, but night full of the flames of burning houses and the fury of conflict.

In the third Act, a sense of desolation gradually succeeds to the strife. Aeneas is left more and more alone, both in responsibility, when with difficulty he persuades his father to join in the escape, and in action, when, having put his father and son in safe hiding outside the smouldering city, he plunges back into it to look for his wife, who had been snatched from him in the escape. Out of all the rejoicing multitude which filled the stage in the first Act, from the smaller but still crowded scenes of combat that made the second, only one man is left. Troy has vanished; the future is with Aeneas alone. And to guide him there is only the faint ray of hope contained in the dubious prophecy of Creusa's ghost, with the geographical contradiction of an Anatolian river [1] in a western

---

[1] That, of course, was the meaning of a *Lydius Thybris* and a *terra Hesperia* to a Trojan ear. Commentators have been too much taken up with the meaning which the words would convey to a Roman to realise that to a Trojan, some generations before the first Etruscan landing in Italy, the prophecy had no meaning except the riddling ambiguity proper to an oracle. I am glad to note that, since this lecture was

land. The story has swept us along swiftly; one vivid picture *cf. Mackail*
has succeeded another too quickly for us to reflect on the constructive art which built them so. To see how powerful this is,
one need only try to remove a single episode from the book.
No episode, hardly even a single line, can be spared; remove it,
and the whole story halts. So, for example, those scholars
have found who wish to reject the passage in which Aeneas de-
bates whether he shall kill Helen. In view of the manuscript
evidence, there can be no doubt that Vergil himself had condemned these lines; [1] but he did not live to rewrite them; and
without them a place in the narrative is left completely blank.
The passages before and after will not fit.

Or again, consider the structure of Book X, the book of
Homeric combats. The commentators have failed to observe
how two scenes of quite different warfare are separated by the
death of Pallas. In the first,[2] Aeneas is on the defensive and
has no particular ardour, though he advances as soon as he sees
the enemy; the story is a series of nine or ten [3] attacks made
upon the Trojans and resisted with difficulty (*anceps pugna
diu*). But as soon as Turnus has slain the boy Pallas, Pallas,
who had been trusted by his aged father Evander to the care
of Aeneas (*Pallas, Euander, in ipsis omnia sunt oculis*), the
warrior's passion is roused, and we have a picture,[4] second to
none in poetry, of the merciless fury of battle, the madness of
the smoking sword. Aeneas giving full play to his revenge is
likened to the hundred-handed Aegeon fighting against Jove,
a significant comparison — all the more because Vergil makes
Aegeon[5] the enemy of Jove, whereas in Homer he is the ally:

> sic toto desaeuit in aequore uictor
> ut semel intepuit mucro.

The last word of the description is *furens*, 'mad' (*torrentis
aquae vel turbinis atri more furens*), which is perhaps the

delivered, the point has been made independently, so far as I know, by Miss Catharine Saunders in the *Classical Quarterly*, XIX (1925), 85.

[1] *Aen.*, II, 567–588.   [2] X, 308–361.

[3] X, 309, 312, 318, 322, 328, 338, 342, 345, 352, 354; the first of the ten represents
the general offensive of the Latins.

[4] X, 512–603.

[5] Horace, *Odes*, III, 4. 49, follows Vergil, but without naming this giant.

briefest, and certainly not the least powerful, of all Vergil's similes. The drama of the book is knit fiercely together, every scene carrying us straight into the next, and the whole sweeping on to the tragic climax in the death of Mezentius. But to this I must return some other day; I will only add now that this whole drama, with its successive pictures of the hero, first hard-pressed by numbers, then irresistible in revenge, then bending in chivalrous pity over the body of his young assailant, and finally winning a hard-fought victory over a dangerous foe, would have been lost if superficial considerations like those of Conington, who counts it a blemish in the story that Pallas and Lausus do not meet, had governed Vergil's design.

If the poet's architectural power is so conspicuous in single Books, we may be sure that it will repay our study in the poem as a whole. At least we may discover some main lines of his plan. And for this there is in our favour one circumstance which otherwise is a great loss — the fact that one of the latest changes Vergil had made in his unfinished poem was in the order of the opening books. One of these (the Third) had been, it now seems, in course of being modified to suit the new order; and it was left so far from complete that it is only in its general design, in the beauty of its versification, and in a few passages of characteristic tenderness, such as the picture of Andromache, and that of Polyphemus with his sheep, that we can call it Vergilian in the full sense;[1] and it was perhaps his consciousness of this gap at an important point which more than anything else led the dying poet to bid his friends destroy the poem. But just for this reason, the order in which he did leave the books is significant, because we know that it repre-

---

[1] On the Third Book I am indebted to a stimulating though not always convincing essay, by Miss M. Crump, on the *Growth of the Aeneid*, Oxford, 1920. Her main contentions regarding the book follow Sabbadini's view, and seem to me justified, although the limits of her essay make the treatment of the other books (especially that of the Twelfth) somewhat cursory. In particular, Miss Crump nowhere reckons with the metrical and other evidence, though both are strong, for the view that some of these Books, especially the Tenth, belong to Vergil's earlier period and are closely akin in style and method to the *Georgics*, especially to the Third Book. My own view, which is, I believe, not new, is that the Tenth Book represents the final form of part of the poem about *reges et proelia* which we know that Vergil contemplated at an early stage (*Ecl.*, VI, 3), say, in 40–37 B.C., and then put aside; though he recurs to it again, in both retrospect and prospect, in *Georg.*, III, 40–49 (in 31 B.C., immediately after the battle of Actium).

sents his mature intention. Some of the implications of this order we may now examine.

We all know that the *Aeneid* contains in itself an Odyssey of travel and an Iliad of war; and it is commonly assumed that the two halves of the poem correspond to this double purpose. This is true on the surface, but only on the surface; there is no travelling in Book II or Book IV — very little (in the geographical sense) in Book VI; and there is no fighting in Book VIII. The chief likeness to the Homeric model is in one detail, namely, of time; the first six books cover seven or eight years, and the last six occupy a certain number of days. This distinction therefore does not take us very far. The questions to which we come now arise out of the maxims that we have noted. How does Vergil secure that the real compass of his poem should not be limited by the experience of Aeneas? How does he contrive to vary the course of his story without interrupting it? How does he secure that the reader shall be conscious throughout of its national and super-national purpose?

To the first question the answer is obvious. In the historical order, Troy comes first, that is to say, Book II; then the wanderings from Troy as far as Sicily, Book III.[1] Then the new start from Sicily, the storm driving the wanderers out of their course, the shipwreck on the Carthaginian coast, the welcome by Dido — all this makes Book I.[2] The tragic love of Dido and Aeneas, the forced departure of Aeneas, and Dido's suicide make Book IV. Then the return to Sicily and the incidents

[1] Here there is a gap. We nowhere learn how Aeneas spent the time between his first landing in Sicily and his starting again on the voyage which ended in his shipwreck. Miss Crump offers a plausible conjecture, that the Funeral Games of Anchises, which, in the poem as we have it, take place a year after his death when Aeneas returned to Sicily, were first designed to occupy this place. There is something to be said for this theory; but the evidence does not yet seem enough to make it more than a question worth further enquiry. If Miss Crump's conjecture were sound, it would render still more noteworthy Vergil's final decision to place Book V where it stands, since it must have involved a great deal of rewriting, as indeed she supposes — but far more rewriting than she has realised. And it would be interesting to see what, say, the first 500 lines of Book III would be like, if they were rewritten now so that every First Person were replaced by a Third Person — a process which Miss Crump thinks "very simple" (p. 35), "not at all difficult" (p. 34). Has she ever tried to write Latin hexameters?

[2] But the Carthaginian pictures of the Trojan War (ll. 454 ff.) look backwards; and the prophecy of Jupiter looks far on to Rome (ll. 254 ff.).

there fill the present Book V. These incidents are important
for the development of the character of Aeneas and for other
reasons, as we shall see; but the main narrative stands still
until the end of the book, when the voyage is begun again —
Palinurus is drowned, but the expedition arrives at Cumae;
then follows the descent to the Underworld in Book VI. But
the events prophesied by Anchises in its latter part relate to
periods that to Aeneas are still in a remote future. Books VII,
X, XI, and XII narrate different stages of the relations of
Aeneas with the Italians, and the repeated breach of their
covenants with him, thanks to Amata and Turnus — the
whole story being concluded by Turnus' death.

The incidents in these four books are connected fairly
closely, except the story of Camilla in the second half of Book
XI;[1] part of this was certainly not composed for that place,
and the episode as a whole might have occurred anywhere
between Book VII and Book XII, though at the end of Book
XI (l. 901) the news of Camilla's death is neatly linked to
what follows in Book XII.

But what of Books VIII and IX? Book VIII narrates the
visit of Aeneas to the site of Rome, where he is taken over
parts of the future area of the city, by the Greek king, Evander, who had settled on the Palatine, and who genially explains
to him the stories connected with each part. Book IX pictures
the events in the Trojan camp, hard pressed by Turnus, during the absence of Aeneas. And we have first the romantic
story of Nisus and Euryalus venturing out by night to try to
recall Aeneas, and so meeting their doom; then the not less interesting pictures of Turnus bursting into the Trojan camp,
shut in there, and fighting his way through to the opposite
wall, whence he plunges armed into the Tiber. All these incidents might have come in anywhere between Book VI and
Book XII, and one episode — the armour made for Aeneas by
Vulcan — includes upon the shield a series of pictures from

---

[1] The speech of Diana (ll. 537-584) clearly comes from some early Epyllion.
Although it is put into Diana's mouth, she is mentioned three times in the third person and never (in these lines) in the first. The number of jingling rhymes in lines
570-576 is remarkable; and the succession of end-stopped lines in 573-580, no less
than their content, is in the manner of Catullus.

Roman history, ending at Actium. If, therefore, we were to arrange these Books by strict chronology, this part would come long after Book XII, and be made parallel to the historical prophecies in Book VI; only that the end of Book VI, the death of Marcellus, which took place in 23 B.C., is later even than the battle of Actium in 31 and the triumphs of Augustus in 29 and 28 B.C. The result may be represented by a string of numbers. In the order of what the books tell us, they would stand thus: II; III; I; IV; V (in its present form); part of VI; VII; VIII, IX, and part of XI (anywhere between VII and XII); X and part of XI; XII; part of VI; part of VIII; part of VI.

The next question goes deeper. How has Vergil contrived to vary his story without interrupting it? One answer lies in the habit of thought traced in a previous lecture,[1] Vergil's way of considering things in pairs, of combining contrasted points of view. His *Eclogues*, we found,[2] are arranged so that those with odd numbers have all Italian subjects, and those with even numbers have subjects beyond Italy. In the *Georgics*, Books I and III have long introductions, of similar [3] length and structure, and no epilogues; but Books II and IV have short introductions, of eight and seven lines respectively, and short epilogues, two lines in Book II, eight in Book IV. The endings of Books I and III are tragic; the last scene of Book II is cheerful and, as it originally stood,[4] so quite certainly was that of Book IV. This same love of alternation has shaped the structure of the *Aeneid* in two ways: (*a*) by the contrast which the poet has made between every pair of consecutive Books, and (*b*) by the correspondence and contrast between each of the Books in the first half of the poem and the Book in the corresponding place in the second half. Take the latter point first.

Book I and Book VII narrate an arrival in a strange land, which proffers friendship at first. Venus prevailing over Juno is the controlling spirit of Book I; Juno prevailing over Venus,

[1] Chapter 7, p. 102.
[2] Chapter 2, p. 16, n. 2.
[3] See Chapter 5, pp. 69 f.
[4] See *Great Inheritance*, chap. 5, "The Fall of Cornelius Gallus."

of Book VII; and both books are full of oracles. Book II and Book VIII tell, each, the story of a city — one doomed, the other yet to be founded; the second to succeed to the glory of the first. In both, the Greeks are the main actors; in Book II they destroy, in Book VIII they help to found. The story of each leaves Aeneas in the centre of the stage. In the next pair the hero is in fact out of the picture, for his part in the narrative of Book III is virtually passive. Both books are crowded with incidents which in Book III centre mainly round the aged Anchises, in Book IX mainly round the young Ascanius. Books IV and X again have, each, the hero in the thick of the action; in Book IV the conflict for him is within, between his duty to the future and his love for Dido; in Book X it is outside, with the Latins and Mezentius. In Book IV private affection yields [1] to public claims; in Book X pity gives place to the stern call of justice. In both, great mischief is done by the interference of divine persons; and in both the strain of tragedy touches its highest point. The central movement of each perceptibly follows the path of Greek drama.

Books V and XI both open with funeral ceremonies. In Book V Aeneas appears as a wise ruler, allaying by his generous sympathy the disputes between his subjects; whereas in Book XI the helpless King Latinus completely fails to avert civil dissension between the two factions of the Latins. In both there is a feminine incursion upon the natural order of events,[2] and both end with the fate of a single personality, the death of Palinurus and the death of Camilla, both slain by some strange law of destiny, demanding, apparently, for any great cause the almost irrelevant sacrifice of innocent lives — *unum pro multis caput*.[3] Finally, Book VI and Book XII show us the founder of Rome first receiving and then executing his commission — first, the revelation of the divine purpose; then, its enactment through the reconciliation of Juno and the covenants of Aeneas. Each Book ends with a death — one, that of Marcellus, consecrating the new order; the other, that of Turnus, sealing the doom of the old. Any pair of these

---

[1] See Chapter 5, pp. 67 f.
[2] Iris in Book V, Camilla in Book XI.
[3] *Aen.*, V, 815; a quite startling coincidence with Hebraic beliefs.

parallel features you may reject as unimportant, if you will; but their number might easily be increased, and, taken together, they seem too substantial a total to be due merely to accident.

Turn now to the alternation in the character of the Books, a point probably familiar to many: the contrast of the grave and the less grave; of a sense of tension and a sense of leisure; a change from tragedy to something which, if not comedy, is at all events melodrama of no very harrowing kind. This is the real division of the *Aeneid*. The books with odd numbers show what we may call the lighter or Odyssean type; the books with the even numbers reflect the graver colour of the *Iliad*. The only point of the *Aeneid* at which this principle may be felt to apply less plainly than in the rest is in Books IX and X. Yet a little reflection will tell us that, although Book IX does indeed contain one story of deep pathos, the fatal adventure of Nisus and Euryalus, nevertheless the atmosphere of the whole book is different from the lurid sky of Book X.

Now observe one effect of this alternation which is especially important for teachers to grasp. We have seen that the epic poet must not break into open laughter, because that would interrupt the serious course of his story; but he may, in suitable places, be playful; he may stoop (or rise) to a smile. In such parts of his work he may watch the actions of young or foolish creatures, not merely with the historian's eye, but with a certain air of sympathy enlivening his judgement; whereas in the more tragic books, if his humour cannot be wholly kept out, it takes a grim form, as in the Sibyl's mocking replies to Aeneas in Book VI, or in the answer which the gods send to the prayer of the confident Tolumnius.[1]

Contrast with this the gentle playfulness that we find colouring the story in the Books with odd numbers. For want of realising this difference, grave commentators have censured the poet for his surprising frivolity; as in the footrace in Book V, where Nisus slips in the mud, but in rising manages to foul Salius so as to leave his friend Euryalus the winner. An incident of this kind, however Homeric, could not have appeared

[1] See Chapter 7, p. 106.

in Book IV or Book VI; nor could the spotted snake with its coat of many colours; or the wise old ladies who burn the ships to escape seasickness; or several other incidents which together make Book V very cheerful reading.

What is it, again, that has made Book I such a favourite in every school all down the centuries? It is just this playful touch which lightens so much of the story. Not the Swiss Family Robinson themselves could have lit on a luckier store of good things than Aeneas' shipwrecked comrades — rescuing plenty of corn from the waves or from their wrecked ships; cooking it on fire kindled from a handy flint; with bows and arrows all ready, and a most obliging troop of stags coming down to be shot; and plenty of wine in casks, unloaded with a speed which would shock Mr. Volstead and excite the envy of many busy persons on the Canadian frontier! And how was the storm raised? By Aeolus, bribed to do so by the promise of a beautiful nymph for his bride. Of course she is Homeric, taken from Book XIV, — the frivolous portion of the *Iliad*, observe, — and it is difficult to think that Vergil wished us to regard her as a very serious element in the fortunes of the founder of Rome. If Aeolus came by a new wife every time he raised a storm, well, he must have had a complicated household, and a very large cave! It is easy to trace this gentle humour in the other books with odd numbers; in Book III the disagreeable but futile Harpies and the muddles of the oracles; in Book VII poor Picus turned into a bird, and the angry old lady Amata spinning about the town so wildly in her fury that she is compared to a top whipped round a courtyard by a crowd of schoolboys; [1] in Book IX the ships prettily and suddenly turned into nymphs, the boyish generosity of Ascanius toward Nisus and Euryalus, his own lucky shot at the declamatory Numanus; and the not less boyish prowess of Turnus, shut up within the walls of the camp. In Book XI we have the high comedy of the debate in the Latin Senate, with Drances for Cicero and Turnus for Antony; and the tragical comedy of poor Camilla pursuing Chloreus for the sake of his fine robes, and so exposing herself to a treacherous arrow.

[1] *Aen.*, VII, 379 ff.

These are obvious examples; but be it added that often, perhaps more often than not, the smile ends in a touch of pathos, sometimes deep pathos, as in the stories of Euryalus and Camilla. Yet unless I am mistaken, the spirit in which these stories as a whole are told hardly appears in the Books with even numbers.[1] And I cannot help feeling that we do not do justice to Vergil in reading any one of his Books, taken alone, unless in our reading we are conscious of this fundamental difference between the two series, those with odd and those with even numbers.

Finally, let me point out what it is that unifies the *Aeneid* in spite of the facts that it is unfinished, and that each of its Books stands out clearly, designed as a separate unit. What is it, nevertheless, that makes the whole a single, complete poem? It is the governing power of its crowning Book, which Vergil has placed in the centre, to unite all that stand before it and all that stand after.

It is half a century since I began to study the *Aeneid*, and I have often had to think about Book VI;[2] yet it is only in the last few years that this effect of it has become clear to my mind. In several different ways the Book contributes a sense of unity to the epic. No doubt we might, to start with, regard the visit of Aeneas to the Underworld as a picturesque but merely incidental episode, which owed its place to the fact that in Homer's story Odysseus had also had dealings with the dead. This, as Heinze suggests, gave an element not very easy to weave into the general plot.[3] All this is true, and yet its truth is a revelation of Vergil's genius, — a measure of the power of imagination which has made it equally true that Book VI is the keystone of the whole poem, — so profound is

---

[1] One clear exception must be admitted — the experiences of the little boy Ascanius at the end of Book II. But in the last Act of that Book, the tension is deliberately relieved; the climax is the death of Priam. The only other exceptions, I believe, that might be urged are in Book X — the vision of Aeneas on his voyage back to the Trojan camp, and the one example of real mockery on the lips of Jove when he reproves Juno for her folly (ll. 608–610). I count these among the many indications of a comparatively early date for the first composition of this Book; see above, p. 136 n.

[2] See, for instance, *Great Inheritance*, chap. 6, "The Growth of the Underworld."

[3] In the *Odyssey*, as we know, it remains a purple patch, or rather two purple patches, hopelessly disconnected from each other, and only loosely connected with the general story. For Heinze's view, see his *Vergils Epische Technik*.

the influence of the Book upon our feelings about what has preceded and what is to follow.

We may note in passing that the frame of the Book is in Italy. Not till he reaches Italy can Aeneas learn the truth; the base of the epic structure must be laid on Italian soil. Then observe that the Book sets the story of Troy and Rome for the first time in the light of universal Providence. It is true that in the First Book, and since, we have had promises and prophecies connecting the Trojan exiles with Rome and giving Aeneas a steadily increasing something both to hope for and to do; yet how small a part is this of the world-drama, or world-procession, which the Sixth Book unfolds! It is not, we now discover, the fate of a few exiles which is at stake; it is the purpose of creation itself; the whole divine ordering of the world from the first stirring of fiery breath in primaeval chaos, from the first imparting of divine life to individual men and other creatures, down to the long process of civilising barbarous humanity; the process of which the Roman Empire was to be the consummation. Seen from such a mount of vision, even the humblest details of the search for a site, of local traditions, of finding allies, of sieges and storms, and single combats — all these incidents are transfigured. In Book VIII it is not merely a picturesque stream in a primaeval forest by which an exile lays him down to sleep and dreams of building a city on its banks: it is the greatest river of human history, 'the source of life,' as Vergil calls it, for many 'tall cities' (*celsis caput urbibus*), rising to its destiny. And later, it is not merely a thieving shepherd from a cave in grassy hills meeting punishment from stronger hands; it is the whole instinct of social order, of moral law, vindicated by the great deliverer, Hercules, against Cacus, and in Vergil's day vindicated against the Catilines, Antonys, and Pompeys who had kept the world in chaos for three generations. And at the end, it is not a mere Italian princeling, resisting the establishment of the new order which everyone else has sworn to welcome, whose death marks the end of the story; it is the whole spirit of no compromise, of "dying hard," of resistance to the last on behalf of merely selfish claims, from which the Roman Empire was freed by the fall of Antony;[1] freed for its work of ensuring peace and of opening the roads along which knowledge and government were to spread. That, and nothing less, is the meaning of the death of Turnus. At both ends of the epic the wall of time is swept away; and the story of Aeneas almost suddenly takes its place in an immortal and infinite Design.

Secondly, if the Sixth Book thus links the poem with universal Providence, it does so by frankly adopting a certain universal philosophy. Whence comes this doctrine of the World-Soul, of the relationship of all life to its spiritual source and goal, of the discipline through which the human soul must pass, the ages over which the creative purpose will range? Certainly not from the Epicurean carelessness or defiant despair by which Vergil's boyish questionings were surrounded. It was the creed of Vergil's mature thought; and it was also [2] the last flowering of Greek philosophy, in a tradition coming down with growing significance from the speculations of the early Ionians to Socrates and Plato, and through them to the Stoics. In their hands, as we know, touched by influence from the East, it became more of a religion than a philosophy, and was closely allied with the fundamental instincts of Roman life. Here let me add only that in linking his poem to Stoic teaching, Vergil did much to bring that teaching into the central current of human progress; and that it was a certain spirit from which, till then, Stoicism had been conspicuously alien, but with which Vergil somehow transfused it, that did more than anything to make that philosophy the natural ally of a new religion.

In the third place, it is obvious that the Book in a sense reveals the secret of the whole poem by linking its dénouement to a central person, namely, Augustus. The conquests of the Caesars had been prophesied before; the religious and social reforms of Augustus had been brightly figured in the dealings of Aeneas with his followers, especially in Book V; but not until

---

[1] Our conception of that fluent ruffian is too much coloured by the tragical stories of his loves. We need to remember what he was after Caesar's death; how he amassed the sum of 700,000,000 sesterces (say, £5,500,000) by selling bogus laws to all parts of the Empire; and how he dictated the Proscription of 43 B.C.

[2] See Chapter 7, p. 108.

the prophecy of Anchises are we told that it is Augustus himself who shall travel through the Empire and make it one, who
shall spread the Golden Age, not only over Italy, but throughout the known world. Henceforward, when we read of the
hard work of Hercules or Aeneas, we know that we are to take
them as an allegory [1] of the harder task to be accomplished by
the founder of the Roman Empire.

We may be sure, I think, that of these three elements in the
Book — a central Providence, a universal philosophy, and a
single person — the poet was conscious; that he deliberately
set it before him to introduce them. But two other things
came in perforce, because they had to, because he could not
help it, because they were part of himself. Both will be by this
time familiar to readers of these lectures.

The first is a certain method, or spirit, the power of which has
brought Aeneas to the Underworld and which will take him
back enlightened, to carry out his mission. It is the Golden
Bough which he discovers amidst the darkness of the forest; [2]
it is the new way of amnesty, 'the custom of peace,' which the
Empire is to take for its governing idea — the conception of
mercy, the central warmth of human affection.

It is this which gives a deeper meaning to the vicissitudes of
the books which follow. Seen in the light of this revelation,
every part of the struggle is irradiate with colours of the dawn.
Nisus and Euryalus must fall, brave and beautiful boys; but
the story of their generous enterprise, their mutual self-sacri-
fice, the honour and affection which they receive from Ascanius and the Trojan elders, and the tragedy of the last scene,
in which the mother of Euryalus beholds their heads impaled
on the enemies' spears and is gently led away into mourning by
honoured commanders in the beleaguered host, the whole
transfused by the depth of Vergil's pity, has won the immortality which he promised; promised indeed in an outburst of
confidence, [3] very rare for him, which marks the temper of
those two boys as the real foundation of the spiritual Rome.

[1] This bold word I owe to my friend Professor D. L. Drew, whose thoughtful
essay on *The Allegory of the Aeneid* has just appeared. I had the privilege of reading
it in manuscript in 1924.
[2] See Chapter 3, p. 48.   [3] *Aen.*, IX, 446-449.

O happy both!   If aught my song avails,
No day shall tear you from remembering years
While by the Capitol's unmoving rock
Aeneas' house shall stand, and he whom Rome
Calls Father, give commandment to the world.

fortunati ambo!   Si quid mea carmina possunt
nulla dies unquam memori vos eximet aevo;
dum domus Aeneae Capitoli immobile saxum
accolet, imperiumque pater Romanus habebit.

Providence, philosophy, person, method — to all these the
Book adds one more supreme uniting power.   On other occasions [1] I have tried to show how Vergil's faith in a well-
meaning Providence was attended everywhere by a sense of
profound mystery; and that even in the final revelation of
Anchises the reader is nowhere allowed to think that he knows
all that we crave to know.   Above all, this sense of mystery
haunts Vergil's choice of a theme for the last scene of the revelation — the crown of the whole triumphant prophecy.   For
this Vergil, with sublime daring, chose the bitterest disappointment that Augustus ever suffered, — a calamity from which
other writers of his age had shrunk away, — the death of the
young Marcellus.   I am constrained to attempt a rough version
of the lines:

> Amid the throng
> Beside him moved a youth of royal mien,
> Clad with bright armour but with joyless eye
> And countenance o'ershadowed.   "Who is he,"
> Aeneas asked, "who follows in such wise
> The train of great Marcellus?   Is't a son,
> Or some remoter scion of his line?"
> How eagerly his comrades round him throng,
> How fair his stature!   But around his head
> Hovers the shade of night on sable wing.
> Then answered him Anchises, through his tears:
> "Seek not to learn the woe of thy descendants.
> The fates will grant men but a moment's sight
> Of that bright star before it sets again.
> Too high the majesty of Rome had towered —
> So ran your thought, ye gods — if men of Rome
> Had boasted such a gift was theirs to keep.
> Hark! from that soldiers' plain, that city of Mars,
> Rises a bitter cry of lamentation.

---

[1] See *Great Inheritance*, chaps. 2 and 6, and Chapter 7 in this volume, p. 112.

What throng of mourning shall thy waters see,
Great Tiber, as they roll beside his grave!
Never on any child of Trojan seed
Shall Latin grandsires build such mighty hope,
None with such pride the land of Romulus bear.
Weep for that loyal heart, that valorous hand;
No foe had e'er encountered him unscathed
When sword to sword he fought, or when with spur
He launched his foaming courser on the fray.
Oh child of sorrow! Were it thine to break
Fate's iron bar, thou should'st, thou shalt be yet
A true Marcellus. Bring me store of lilies,
Come, fill your hands with bluebells of the spring;
So let me crown my son, tho' vain the honour;
Crown him,[1] and leave the issue."

The Sixth Book deals with death, we know, and therefore such an end is fitting. Fitting indeed, but what does it mean? From the wistfulness of its opening question,

> tantaene animis caelestibus irae?

to the pathos of its closing note, of pity even for Turnus, the story of the *Aeneid*, like the whole of human life, to Vergil is shadowed by mystery; and this mystery unites every part of the story, just as it unites every person, every creature, under the spell of our mortal condition. And why was that funeral picture, with its terrible memories, so welcome to Augustus and his sister, the bereaved mother, that no wealth or honour they could heap upon the poet seemed to them great enough thanks? And why, though to us Marcellus is only the name of a prince who died before his time, why has this passage been counted always among the most golden lines of all inspired speech? Because the mystery that it celebrates united Augustus with his subjects in the glow of their sympathy; because it told him that, though he was an emperor, yet he was not alone; though he was an emperor, yet the powers of life could deal him as fierce a blow as the meanest of his subjects could suffer; though he was an emperor, he could find comfort, the only comfort, for such a grief, in the human affection to which the meanest of his subjects must turn when the dark day came. And in thus linking the mystery of death with the power of

---

[1] This half-line attempts to express the meaning of *saltem*.

human love, the Sixth Book of the *Aeneid* has not merely united the whole of that poem into a great forecast of the Christian good tidings: it has bound its author by the strongest tie to the heart of every reader through all the generations that came and are to come.

> He saw afar the immemorable throng,
> And bound the scattered ages with a song.[1]

Human genius, at its highest, overpasses mortal bars. Vergil's vision is not of the Augustans, but of all time; his faith is not Roman, but cosmic. His epic is both an image and a part of life. Its architecture springs from the ultimate foundations: its pillars are pillars of the world.

[1] "The Sovereign Poet" (Sir William Watson, *Odes and Other Poems*).

INDICES

I. INDEX OF PROPER NAMES

Abbott, Dr. Edwin A., 130.
Aberdeen, 129.
Actium, 54, 59, 69, 109, 136, 139.
Adamello, Mt., 30.
Aegeon, 135.
Aeneas, 67, 100, 104, 134, 135, 140, 145.
Aeolus, 142.
Africa, invaded, 114.
Agrigentum, 83.
Albius Calenus, 122.
Alcinous, 132.
Alexander the Great, 117.
Alfenus Varus, 33, 36.
Allucius, 123.
Amata, 138, 142.
Amphrysus, 69.
Anaxagoras, 97.
Anchises, 47, 66, 106, 107, 110.
Ancyranum, Monumentum, 54.
Anderson, W. B., 14, 19, 38.
Andes, 14, 18, 29.
Andicus, 36, 38.
Andromache, 136.
Antiochus, 24, 119.
Antiphon, 96.
Antony, Mark, 3, 4, 36, 50, 59, 60, 125, 142, 144-145.
Apollo, Phoebus, 69, 78, 80.
Apollonius Rhodius, 25, 133.
Appian, 3.
Appian Way, 9.
Aratus, 71.
Arcadia, 69.
Archimedes, 62.
Arden, Enoch, 130.
Aricia, 41.
Aristotle, 97.
Armenia, 70.
Arnold, E. V., 102.
Ascanius, 106, 110, 142.
Ashburner, Walter, 22.
Asia Minor, 80.
Asola, 22.
Asselia Sabina, 21, 24.
Atellae, 79.
Athens, 95.
Atkinson, Donald, 14, 73.
Atrius Umber, 120.
Augustus, 37, 47, 54, 125, 145. *See also* OCTAVIAN.

Bacchus, 80, 95.
Balder, 43, 44.
Balzo, Sign., 22.
Becula, 123.
Benacus, suffix of, 38.
Benn, A. W., 96.
Benn, Mrs. A. W., 15.
Bernese Scholiast, 33.
Betriacum, 40.
Bianor, 22.
Bishop Blougram, 130.
'Black and Tans,' 83.
Braunholtz, G. E. K., 14.
Brescia, 15, 19, 22, 29, 32.
Britain, 5, 70.
Brixia, 14, 19.
Bruttians, 83.
Brutus, M. Iunius, 4, 111.
Bubulcus, 58.
Bunyan, 48.
Butcher, S. H., 71.

Cacus, 144.
Caesar, C. Iulius, 4, 11, 17, 60, 125.
Caesar Augustus. *See* AUGUSTUS.
Calabria, 37.
Calder, W. M., 14.
Calvisano, 19, 20, 21, 22, 30, 31, 32, 39.
Camilla, 101, 138, 140, 142.
Cannae, 61, 74, 77; 'soldiers of,' 89.
Capitol, 117.
Capua, 76, 79, 115.
Caracallus, 60.
Carli, Prof., 17.
Carpenedolo, 17, 27, 30, 31, 39.
Carthage, 137.
Carthage, New, 116, 123.
Carthaginians, 123.
Casalpoglio, 21, 39.
Cassia Secunda, 21, 39.
Cassiodorus, 58.
Cassius, 4.
Castiglione, 22.
Catalepton, 15.
Catiline, 144.
Catius Callaui f., 40.
Catulla, Munatia, 20.
Catullus, 138.
Censors, 90.
Centaurs. *See* Lapithae.

Charon, 46, 106.
Cheiron, the Centaur, 25.
Chicago, 130.
Chiese (the ancient *Clesis*), 21, 30, 31, 39.
Chloreus, 142.
Cicero, 5, 7, 142.
Ciris, 64.
Cirta, 124.
Claudius, 85.
Cleopatra, 125.
Colline Gate, 78, 115.
Commentary of Servius, 36.
Comte, Auguste, 72.
Conington, John, 95, 136.
Coriolanus, 113.
Cornelius, orator, 33.
Cornelius Gallus, 32, 34, 35, 36, 64, 71.
Crassus, 36.
Cremona, 15, 19, 26, 28, 31.
Crete, 64.
Creusa, 100.
Crispinus, T. Quinctius, 61, 83.
Crump, Miss M., 136.
Culex, 49, 63, 70, 71.

Dante, 15, 22, 97, 130.
Decemvirs, 78.
Delphi, 78.
Detlesson, 56.
Deucalion, 16.
Diana, 138.
Diana Nemorensis, 41.
Dido, 67, 71, 98, 104, 111, 125.
Dio Cassius, 60.
Diomede, 132.
Dis, 45.
Domitius Calvinus, 60.
Donatus, 38, 49.
Drances, 111, 142.
Drew, D. L., 17, 38, 49, 146.
Dryads, 95.

Eclogue, Fourth, etc. *See* Index III.
Edda, 45.
Egnatius, 36.
Elizabeth, Queen, 75.
Elysium, 110.
Ennius, 81.
Enoch Arden, 130.
Epicurus. *See* Index II, *s. v.* Philosophy.
Etruria, 79.
Etruscan, 24, 134.
Euryalus, 100, 110, 138, 141, 143, 146.

Evander, 104, 110, 135, 138.
Evans, Sir A., 64.

Fabius Maximus Cunctator, Q., 61, 81, 86, 118.
Fabius Pictor, 78.
Fasti Capitolini, 59, 61.
Fauns, 95.
Filargyrius, 18.
Flaccus (brother of Vergil), 37.
Floronia, 78.
Fondo Virgiliano, 29.
Fowler, W. Warde, 10, 14, 49, 54, 64, 66, 77, 80.
Frazer, Sir James, 41 ff.
Frusino, 79.

Gala, 124.
Galaesus, 15, 110.
Gallus, Cornelius, 32, 34, 35, 36, 64, 71.
Gauls, 57, 90.
Garibaldi, 93.
Gellius, 35, 118.
Georgics. See Index III.
Germanicus, 21.
Geta, 60.
Giants, 69.
Giorgione, 113.
Glaucon, 132.
Greene, W. C., 100.

Hallam, G. H., 27, 31.
Hannibal, 61, 115, 122.
Harpies, 142.
Hasdrubal, 76, 85, 124.
Hasta, 21.
Hebe, 53.
Hector, 134.
Hegel, 94, 97.
Heinze, R., 143.
Helen, 135.
Hellespont, 118.
Henzen, W., 58.
Herbert, Mary, 40.
Herdonea, 90, 92.
Herennius, 7.
Hesiod, 37.
Hesperia, terra, 134.
Hirtius, 4.
Holland, Philemon, 122.
Homer, 65, 97, 130, 132 f.
Horace, 54, 55, 98, 110.
Hostilia, 18.
Huelsen, C., 38.
Hyginus, 71.

Iliad, 130, 132.
India, 70.
Inferno, Dante's, 97.
Ionians, 145.
Iris, 140.
Isaiah, 51.
Italy, 144.

Jahn, Otto, 38.
Jonson, Ben, 40.
Jucundus, 23.
Julia, daughter of Augustus, 50.
Julius Caesar, dictator, 4, 11, 17, 60, 125.
Junius Bubulcus, C., 58.
Juno, 104, 111, 139.
Jupiter, 53, 78, 105, 133.
Jupiter incarnate, 43.
Juturna, 111.

Keil, H., 38.
Kipling, Rudyard, 130.

Laelius, C., 116, 124.
Laevinus, 83.
Laocoön, 101, 134.
Lapithae, 69.
Latins, 140.
Latinus, King, 110, 140.
Lausus, 100, 110, 136.
Lavinia, 98, 105, 111.
Lechi, Count, 14, 17, 31, 39.
Lepidus, M. Aemilius, 3, 4, 8, 11.
Livius (Consul in 207 B.C.), 86.
Livy, 61, 62, 73, 75, 78, 113.
Lucina (goddess), 52.
Lucretius, 65, 71.
Locri, 84.
Loki, 45.
Lycurgus, 115.
Lydius Thybris, 134.

Mackail, J. W., 51.
Mackenzie, J. S., 99.
Macrobius, 38.
Maecenas, 34, 36, 37, 55, 70.
Maesulii, 124.
Magia, gens, 19, 21, 36, 38.
Magia Polla, 36.
Magia Procula, 38.
Magius, C., 38.
Magius, P., 21, 40.
Manchester, 130.
Manilius (astronomer), 71.

Mantovana, villa, 22.
Mantua, 14, 17, 29, 31, 39, 68, 70.
Marcellus, M. Claudius (died 208 B.C.), 61 f., 79, 83, 84, 89, 91, 92.
Marcellus, M. Claudius (died 23 B.C.), 111, 140, 147.
Marcia, 79.
Marcius, 86.
Mars, 133.
Martial, 68.
Masinissa, 124.
Massiva, 123.
Matronae (Keltic deities), 20.
Medole, 40.
Meliboeus, 17, 26, 27, 34.
Mella (river), 31.
Menalcas, 17, 25, 26, 28, 34.
Menoetes, 110.
Metaurus, 76, 86, 87.
Mezentius, 136, 140.
Michael Angelo, 56.
Milan, 15.
Milennius, 9.
Miles Standish, 130.
Milo, 11.
Milton, 48, 130, 131.
Mincius (river), 17, 26, 31, 39.
Minerva, 95.
Mingazzini, P., 56.
Minturnae, 79.
Misenus, 42.
Moeris, 34, 35.
Mommsen, Theodor, 10, 14, 18, 19, 23, 38, 54, 58.
Montechiari, 30.
Monumentum Ancyranum, 54.
Munatia, 20.
Munro, H. A. J., 15.
Murray, Gilbert, 133.
Mutina, 4.
Mutinense, bellum, 34.

Naiads, 69.
Nardi, Sign., 36.
Naviglio, 31.
Nemi, 41, 43.
Neptune, 100, 116.
Nettleship, H., 15, 18, 38.
New England, 75.
Nissen, H., 18.
Nisus, 100, 110, 138, 141, 146.
Norden, E., 37, 38, 45, 51, 111.
Numanus, 142.
Numidia, 125, 127.

Octavian, 3, 4, 14, 26, 34, 37, 47, 50, 54, 55, 59, 60, 68, 69. *See also* AUGUSTUS.
Octavius, 3, 69.   *See further* OCTAVIAN *and* AUGUSTUS.
Octavius Musa, 19, 34.
Odysseus, 97, 132, 143.
Opimia, 78.
Orpheus, 71.
Ostiglia, 18.
Ovid, 133.

Pacedianus, 23, 25.
Page, T. E., 64.
Palatine, 138.
Pales, 69.
Palinurus, 138, 140.
Pallas (son of Evander), 98, 101, 110, 111, 135, 136.
Pallas Athene, 100.
Pamphilus, 24.
Pan, 95.
Panaetius, 81.
Pansa, 4.
Paribeni, Prof., 56.
Paris, 105.
Parthia, 70.
Peacock, J., 40.
Pharsalia, 11.
Philologus, 7.
Phoebus Apollo, 69, 78, 80.
Picus, 142.
Pietole, scenery of, 17, 19, 20, 22, 23, 25, 29, 39.
Pindar, 111.
Plato, 52, 97, 145.
Pliny, 52.
Plutarch, 7.
Pollio, 17, 32, 33, 34, 36.
Polybius, 81, 114, 115, 119, 122.
Polyphemus, 25, 136.
Pompey, Cn., 11, 36, 144.
Pompey, Sextus, 9.
Pompilius, 7.
Pomponius, 8.
Prescott, H. W., 45.
Priam, 134.
Probus, 34, 35.
Proculus, 37.
Propertius, 15, 68.
Proserpine, 42, 71.
Psalms, 99.
Pyrrha, 16.
Pyrrhus, 134.

Quintilian, 28.
Quintilius Varus, 26, 34, 35, 37.

Ramsay, W. M., 38.
Rand, E. K., 34, 49.
Regia, 56, 57, 60.
Remulus, 101.
Restio, 8.
Rhegium, 83.
Ribbeck, O., 38.
Ribchester, 60 n.
Ridgeway, Wm., 45.
Roman Empire, 144.
Rome, 137, 138, 144.
Rostra, the, 8.

Sabbadini, Prof., 136.
Sabbia, Val, 30.
Sabinus, name in Vergilian family, 23, 24.
Saintsbury, Prof. G., 105.
Salapia, 84.
Salian Priest, 118.
Salius, 141.
Satan, 122, 132.
Satria Tertia, 21, 39 f.
Satrian House, 21, 40.
Saturn, 52.
Saunders, Catharine, 135.
Schanz, M., 38.
Scholiasta Bernensis, 33.
Scipio, P. Cornelius, Africanus, 74, 87, 92, 114 f., 123.
Scipio Aemilianus, 78, 81.
Scipio, Lucius, 116.
Scipionic circle, 80, 114.
Scipios, the, 76, 80 f., 86, 114.
Seeley, J. R., 130.
Sempronius, 84 f.
Servius, 33, 42, 43.
Severus, 60.
Shakespeare, 3, 16.
Shuckburgh, E. S., 115.
Sibyl, the, 46, 47, 106, 141.
Sibylline Books, 78.
Sicily, 61, 83, 92, 93.
Silenus, 71.
Silvanus, 95.
Silvia, 110, 111.
Sinon, 134.
Siro, 15, 29.
Skutsch, Franz, 16, 64.
Slater, D. A., 64, 133.

Socrates, 97, 145.
Sophonisba, 124, 127.
Spain, 82, 86, 114, 115, 118.
Spenser, 48.
Stoics. *See* Index II, *s. v.* Philosophy.
Strabo, 71.
Sucro, 119.
Sulla, 6.
Syphax, 124, 126.
Syracuse, 61, 83.

Tacitus, 60.
Tarentum, 15.
Tartarus (river), 23.
Tempest, The, 64.
Tennyson, 98, 130.
Terence, 81.
Theocritus, 25.
Thilo, G., 33, 34, 37, 38.
Tiber, 134, 148.
Tiberius, 14.
Titian, 113.
Tityrus, 26, 27, 34.
Tolumnius, 106, 141.
Torquatus, 111.
Trasimene, 61, 74, 77.
Trebia, 61, 74.
Troy, 134, 144.
Tucca, 37.
Turia, 4 ff.

Turnus, 65, 98, 101, 105, 111, 135, 138, 142.

Valeggio, 38, 39.
Valerius Maximus, 4.
Valerius Probus, 18.
Valerius Proculus, 38.
Varro, 37, 59, 71.
Varus, Quintilius, 26, 34, 35, 37.
Vaughan, C. E., 25.
Veii, 79.
Veneti, Veneticus, 38.
Ventidius, 9.
Venus, 48, 100, 104, 111, 139.
Vergil. *See* Index III.
Vergilius, M., 24.
Verona, 18, 19, 23, 31.
Vesta, 57.
Vibo Valentia, 24.
Vicenza, 31.
Vispullo, Q. Lucretius, 4, 9, 11, 12.
Volsci, 38.
Volstead, 142.
Vulcan, 133, 138.

Watson, William, 149.
Wordsworth, 107.

Zama, 74, 93, 114.
Zoroaster, 52.

II. INDEX OF TOPICS

acies, Derbyshire 'edge,' 64.
Adoption at Rome, 12.
Adventure, spirit of, 97.
Aeneid, plan of, 129 ff., 133, 136, 141.
See further Index III.
Affection, natural, 47 f.
Alexandrian school of poetry, 51 f., 69, 133.
Allegories, in Vergil, 45, 144, 146.
Alps, seen from Calvisano, 30.
Alternation, Vergil's love of, 16 n., 139, 141.
American life, 97.
Animals, small, 50, 110.
Answers to prayer, 48, 106, 141.
Antithesis in thought, 97 ff.
antrum in the Eclogues, 25, 27.
Armour, captive, 98.
Augur, augury, 106.
augustus, 54.
Autobiography of Augustus, 54; in Vergil, 32 ff., 108 n.

Balder the Beautiful, 43.
Bee-breeding, 100, 102.
Beech trees, group of, 25, 28.
Bellum Mutinense, 37.

Calendar, 56.
Canticles sung at Rome, 79.
Causation, double, 47, 65, 100; natural, 100; internatural, 100; supernatural, 100.
Celestial debate, 104.
Chaos, 97.
Child of promise, 51 f.
Chivalry of Scipio, 123.
Christianity, forecast of, in Vergil, 149.
Chronology, of the *Eclogues*, 32 ff.; of the *Aeneid*, 137; of Roman history, 55 f., 59.
College of Pontiffs, 77, 79.
Colonies, in revolt, 88.
Commentaries, ancient, on Vergil, 33 ff.
Compromise, at Rome, 88.
Compulsory service, 90.
Confiscations, 5, 19 n., 26, 32 f.
Conscientious objectors, 75, 91.
Conscription at Rome, 90.
Contemporary allusions in Livy, 125.

Cozening of Jove, 133.
Crowns in Elysium, 110.
Crucifixion, 84.

Daring of Vergil, 147.
Dedications, 20.
Deification of emperors, 68 f.
deus, 71.
Divination, 77.
Divorce at Rome, 12.
Dogma and experience, 80.
Double causation, 47, 65, 100.
Double statement, 99.
Doves of Venus, 48.
Dualism of contrast, 102 f.

Epic, definition of, 130, 133.
Episodes in epic poetry, 133, 138.
Epitaphs, 3, 39 f.
Epyllia, 69, 71, 133, 138 n.
Erasure of names on inscriptions, 59 f.
Ethics, Vergil's contribution to, 68, 111 f.
European War (1914–18), the, 73 ff., 80, 109.
Exploration, love of, 97.
Expurgatory theory, 133.

Fasti, Consulares, 56, 58, 61; *Triumphales*, 57.
Fate, 101 f.
Fighting in the *Aeneid*, 135.
Financial strain, 75, 82.
Fire to the ships, 107.
First person, forms of, 121.
Folk-lore, 41 f., 45, 95.
Forgiveness, 50.
Forum Romanum, 56.
Frankness of Livy, 113.
Fraudulent use of religion, 118.
Funeral Games, 104, 107, 140.

Games in *Aeneid*, Book V, 104, 107.
genius loci, 66.
gens Magia, 21.
gens Vergilia, 21 f.
Ghosts, 49 f.
God, the English word, 72.
Golden Age, 47, 50, 146.
Golden Bough, 41 ff., 48, 112, 146.
Golden Mean, 97 f.

Hebraic beliefs, 140; style, 99.
Hebrew prophets, 50.
Hesitation between alternatives in Vergil, 65 f., 71.
Homeric lays, 132.
Homeric matter, 65, 142 f.
Human sacrifice, 78.
Humanity, of Livy, 124 ff.; of Scipio, 123 ff.; of Vergi,l 50 ff., 109 ff., 148.

Imagination, Livy's, 114, 128.
Immortality, 112, 148 f.
Imperator, the title, 125.
Inscriptions, Latin, discussed, 3 f., 14 n., 19 n., 20, 21 f., 23 f., 39 f., 55 f., 59 f., 61.
International causation, 100.
Irrigation, 25.

Jewish scriptures, 99.
Justice, the Maid, 52.

King of the Wood, 41 f.
Kingship, oriental, 125, 127; spiritual and secular, 42 f.

Laughter, in poetry, 133.
Lettering as evidence of date, 21.
Love and Strife, 97.
Lovingkindness of Vergil, 110, 148.

Machines of Archimedes, 62.
Masks, sacred, 95.
Messianic hopes, 50 f.
Metamorphosis of Ovid, 133.
milites Cannenses, 89 f.
Mind and Chaos, 97.
Miracles, told of Scipio, 117.
Mistletoe, 43 f.
Moral law, 102 n., 144.
Motives in the Aeneid, 111.
Munitions, supply of, 75.
Mutiny at Sucro, 120.
Mystery, sense of, in Vergil, 32, 98 f., 147 f.
Mysticism, 99.

Narration, retrospective, 132.
National character, 81, 113.
National consciousness, 75 f., 113.
National purpose of the Aeneid, 137.
Nature, laws of, 102 n.; bounty of, 109.
Nomenclature, Roman, 20.
Numeral signs, 55 n.

Oak, sacred, 44, 45 n.
ob patriam, 110.
Odyssean type of story, 141.
Olympus, debate in, 104.
Omens, 48, 66, 77, 79, 101, 106 f., 120.
Oracle of Delphi, 78.
Oracles, Scipio's use of, 115.
Oratorical power of Livy, 123.
oscilla, 95.

Paradox, of love, 111.
Pastoral style, 51.
Patriotism, 82.
Persian Wars, 69.
Philosophy, Platonic, 52, 71, 97; Zoroastrian, 52; Epicurean, 95; ethical, 68, 97, 102 n.; Stoic, 81, 102, 108 f., 145; of Vergil, 93 ff., 109, 111 f., 145.
pietas, 47.
Piety of Aeneas, 47; of Scipio, 117 f.
Playfulness of Vergil, 141 f.
Poison, use of, 127.
Pontifex maximus, 24, 56.
Prayer, answered, 48, 106, 141.
Precedents, treatment of, 86.
Preface, Livy's, to Punic War, 75.
pro patria, 110.
Prodigies, 77.
Prologues, Vergilian, 69, 139.
Prophecy, 77, 146.
Proscription of 43 B.C., 3, 5 ff.
Providence, 102, 144.
Psychology, modern, 117; of a crowd, 121; of laughter, 133.
Public opinion at Rome, 86 f.
publica opinio, 42.

Rain of stones, 79.
Reforms of Augustus, 145.
religio, 78.
Religious experience, Roman, 77.
Republic, weakness of, 114.
Revelation of Anchises, 47.
Rex nemorensis, 41 f.
Roman Empire, as the design of Providence, 144.
Roman virtues in Livy, 113.

Sacred Spring, 78.
Salian priesthood, 118.
Scenery of N. Italy, 17, 26, 27, 29 f., 37.
Scipionic circle, 81, 114.
Self-control, 96, 98.
Serpents, 51, 66, 142.

Sheep-dipping, 103.
Sibylline Books, 78.
Sicilian colour in Vergil, 25 n.
Signet ring, 83.
Signs, numeral, 55 n.; for English pound and Italian lira, 55 n.
Slaves, in Elysium, 110.
Slave-soldiers (Volones), 84 f.
Snakes, 51, 66, 142.
σωφροσύνη, 96.
Spanish Wars, 75.
Stag, Silvia's, 110.
Statues in the Regia, 60.
Suffixes, local, 38.
Super-self-confidence, 118 f., 122.
Swallows and bees, 102.

Time in the *Aeneid*, 137.
Topics rejected by Vergil, 69 f.

Townships, modern attribution of Italian, 22 n.
Tragedy, Greek, 97; in Vergil, 140.
Translation, inadequacy of, 63 n.
Triumph, Roman, 52.
Triumvirate of 43 B.C., 4 f.
Trojan legend, 70.

Underworld, 41, 46, 49, 66, 70 f., 110.
Unfinished character of the *Aeneid*, 136.

Vestal Virgins, 78.
Violentia, 98.
Volones, 84 f.

War of Independence, 75.
Wolf, as an omen, 79.
Wonder, habit of, 97 f.
World War. *See* European War.
World-soul, 108.

III. LIST OF PASSAGES FROM VERGIL DISCUSSED OR CITED

Aeneid
I, l. 2; 99.
  72; 142.
  254 ff.; 137.
  382; 102.
  454 ff.; 137.
  571; 99.
  603; 102.
  709–710; 102.
  742; 71.
II, l. 34; 102.
  54; 101.
  200; 101.
  212; 101.
  228; 101.
  244; 101.
  336; 102.
  567–588; 135.
  603–616; 100.
  683; 106.
  723; 107.
  738–739; 66, 100.
  781; 134.
III, l. 22; 45.
  150; 102.
  172, 102.
  262; 66, 100.
  331–332, 102.
IV, ll. 156–159; 107.
  315–316; 100.
  327–330; 67.
  352; 102.
  354; 102.
  361; 67.
  625–629; 75.
  696; 102.
V, l. 89; 104.
  95; 66.
  189; 104.
  229; 104.
  235; 104.
  341; 104.
  354; 104.
  383; 104.
  413; 104.
  667; 108.
  671; 107.

Aeneid (continued)
V, l. 815; 140.
VI, gen.; 71.
  l. 20; 64.
  129; 46.
  136; 42.
  137; 41.
  190; 48, 102
  193; 102.
  204; 41, 48.
  209; 45.
  304; 106.
  660–665; 110.
  688; 47.
  718; 109.
  733; 109.
  846; 75.
  859; 75.
  861; 147.
  868; 109.
  869; 111.
VII, gen.; 110.
  l. 379 ff.; 142.
  423; 98.
  483; 111.
  503; 110.
  535; 110.
  695; 64.
VIII, l. 65; 144.
  678; 54.
IX, l. 184; 66, 100.
  254; 102.
  446–449; 146.
  601; 101.
  744; 102.
X, gen.; 135.
  l. 18; 104.
  62–95; 105.
  109–110; 66, 100.
  203; 24.
  308–361; 135.
  309; 135.
  312; 135.
  318; 135.
  322; 135.
  328; 135.
  331; 100.

Aeneid (continued)
X, l. 338; 135.
  342; 135.
  345; 135.
  352; 135.
  354; 135.
  433; 101.
  502; 98.
  512–603; 135.
  515; 135.
  570; 135.
  604; 135.
  608–610; 143.
XI, l. 118; 102.
  336; 111.
  537–584; 138.
  573–558; 138.
  901; 101, 138.
XII, l. 27; 98.
  222; 102.
  228; 102.
  259; 106.
  461; 106.
  517; 110.
  554; 102.
  560; 102.
  862–868; 101.
  894–895; 101.
  895; 98.
  913–917; 102.
  931; 98, 101.
  944; 111.
  952; 65.
Catalepton
  X, gen.; 15, 29.
Ciris
  gen.; 64.
Culex
  gen.; 49.
  ll. 1–11; 69.
  1–40; 63.
  381; 50.
Eclogues
  gen.; 16, 17, 32.
I, l. 6; 68.
  16; 101.
  22; 27.

Eclogues (*continued*)
I, ll. 35–36; 27.
  46; 26.
  69; 27.
  75; 27.
  84; 27.
II, gen.; 28.
  l. 21; 16.
III, gen.; 17, 28.
  l. 111; 25.
IV, gen.; 16, 35, 50.
  partly transl.; 52.
  l. 5; 35.
  12; 35.
  17; 51.
  18; 52.
  21; 52.
  23; 52.
  29; 35.
  43–45; 52.
  49; 51.
  52; 35.
  60; 52.
  61; 51.
  63; 51.
V, gen; 17 35, 37.
  l. 6; 25.

Eclogues (*continued*)
V, l. 8; 25.
  63; 25.
  86–87; 28.
VI, gen; 16.
  l. 3; 136.
  6; 33.
VII, gen.; 17.
  l. 56, 58; 26.
VIII, l. 21; 16.
IX, gen.; 17, 26, 32.
  l. 5; 34.
  6; 34.
  7; 19.
  7 ff.; 38.
  7–10; 28.
  10; 33.
  11; 33.
  12; 34.
  14; 108.
  27; 35.
  27–29; 26.
  29; 35.
  30–31; 35.
  46–50; 35.
  59; 38.
  60; 22.

Eclogues (*continued*)
IX, l. 67; 35.
  72; 34.
X, gen.; 16.

Epitaph, 37.

Georgics
I, gen.; 65.
  l. 11 ff.; 95.
  24–42; 63, 69.
  36–42; 70.
  272; 103.
  500–503; 68.
II, ll. 198–202; 39.
  199; 117.
  200; 39.
  207–211; 103.
  380–396; 95.
  433; 110.
  490; 65.
  523; 110.
III, ll. 1–48; 69.
  40–49; 136.
IV, l. 17; 102.
  125; 15.
  563; 33.